Properly ID'D
Adapting Your Mindset to Your God-sized identity

Edited by

Dr. Yasha Jones Becton

Published by Wysdom Central Publications, LLC
Columbia, South Carolina
Email: wysdomcentralpubs@gmail.com

Printed in the United States of America

DEDICATION

This book is dedicated to Apostle Gary Becton and God's End Time Warriors Apostolic Ministries. "For the vision is yet for an appointed time, but at the end it shall speak, and not lie: though it tarry, wait for it; because it will surely come, it will not tarry." Habakkuk 2:3 KJV

This book is also dedicated to the women of God that have shared in this divinely inspired work: Kristen Baker, Yasha Jones Becton, Ebony Green, Kylie McBride, Shawn Moreland, and Gertrude Thompson. "And he gave some, apostles; and some, prophets; and some, evangelists; and some, pastors and teachers; For the perfecting of the saints, for the work of the ministry, for the edifying of the body of Christ: Till we all come in the unity of the faith, and of the knowledge of the Son of God, unto a perfect man, unto the measure of the stature of the fullness of Christ." Ephesians 4:11-13 KJV

TABLE OF CONTENTS

FOREWORD

One of the greatest disappointments as a Pastor is to see the lack of spiritual growth and maturity among many of today's Christians. Approximately three (3) years ago in a time of prayer and seeking the Lord for direction and guidance for the church that I had been pastoring for a little over six (6) years at the time God said to me, "They won't grow until they know." After a few follow-up questions from me and responses from God, I came to understand that the knowing He spoke of involved proper identity. Too many of us are clueless when it comes to knowing who we are in God.

This then took me back to my high school basketball coach who led us to our first state championship in almost twenty (20) years. He would always emphasize to us the importance of knowing who we were as a team and not to be overly concerned about the opposition. Not a lot of time was spent analyzing or profiling the other team, but he made sure that we would be intensely focused on understanding who we were and our plan for the next opponent in every way both individually and collectively as a team. This life philosophy made us believe that we could handle anyone or anything that happened in our lives and on the basketball court.

We know the importance of reaching the lost at any cost and aggressively going after new souls for Christ. However, I've come to realize that until we who are already part of the Kingdom understand who we are in Christ, we will never step into our God-sized identity to fulfill our true purpose. Hence, why many of us perpetually come up short of the mark. God told Gideon, "Go in the strength you have" (Judges 6:14 NIV). Notice not the strength I will give you, the strength waiting for you or the strength that has been promised, but the "strength" that you already have. If you are a born-again believer God has already properly ID'D you by His Holy Spirit that is in you.

If you have His Holy Ghost living in you, you have already been Properly ID'D! Now it's time to Adapt Your Mindset to Your God-sized identity.

Properly ID'D: Adapting Your Mindset to Your God-sized identity should be required reading for every Christian. If you already know who you are it's time for you to help someone else with their identity crisis. Your spiritual life is to be more than consuming everything you can from the buffet table of religious experiences and never pouring into someone else.

However, let me warn you. If you are looking for just another how-to manual, you've picked up the wrong book. This is a God-inspired, anointed, life-breathing instrument God will use as a turning point to move you to the proven lane of spiritual maturity and purpose; providing you cooperate with His plan. Do the work and see the results.

I've known Dr. Yasha Jones Becton for over twenty (20) years and she and her team have put together a "Word" based, cognitive work to bless the Kingdom of God. *This is the right book at the right time!*

Pastor Ted Pasley
Restoration Life Ministries
Columbia, South Carolina

INTRODUCTION

Wysdom Central Publications, LLC was birthed out of a need for more Biblically sound study material for churches that minister to a diverse demographic. Since I was a child, I have always loved Sunday School. And I am not ashamed to say that I Pastor a church that still does Sunday School on Sunday morning. As believers, we are given the opportunity to increase immeasurably when we participate in a systematic study of the Word of God. Sunday School and Wednesday Night Bible Study have provided rich experiences for us to delve deeper into the study of God's Word as well as create an environment for questions and authentic fellowship. As a Pastor, I'm also frequently asked to recommend good Christian reading material for individuals wanting to enhance their personal devotional time with a spiritual, yet relevant, Bible Study. Lately, this has been somewhat of a challenge. Within the challenge, I found a renewed call to be the change I was desperately searching for.

Properly Id'd is designed to serve all of the needs aforementioned while addressing one of the rather sensitive and under-discussed topics in the church – spiritual identity. From the time we are born (in the natural), we have to address issues of identity immediately. When you have a baby, there is certain information that you must provide the hospital prior to leaving the facility. For example, you may be asked to share the child's name, the father's name and birthplace, as well as the mother's name and birthplace. Identity becomes an immediate and urgent matter. The same is true as it relates to spiritual matters. It is critical that we understand who we are as it relates to our heavenly calling. Who does God see when He looks at you? What name has He given you? What did God have in mind when He created you? Don't you want to know? If you're uncertain, it is very possible for you to know.

As we study Judges the 6th chapter and look into the life of Gideon, we explore the issue of Kingdom Identity. For this study, there are three primary tools that we utilize to take you on this journey.

1. **The Word** –We focus on the Word of God. While you will in no way need a theology degree to read or understand this book, we intentionally highlight and explain the Word of God. We are entrusting you with a narrative derived from the Word of God in hopes that you will be stirred to go back to the Word of God for further and deeper revelation.

2. **Life-Sustaining Principles** –We also make a conscious attempt to highlight what we call Life-Sustaining Principles. The LSPs are principles that will ensure consistency for the changed life. In other words, principles that will keep you on the right path.

3. **Reflective Questions** – The third and final tool is a set of reflective questions at the end of each chapter. This book is designed to prompt you to reflect or think. It is our prayer that upon reading this book from beginning to end, you will be able to definitively and clearly describe (to anyone) who you are in the Kingdom.

It is our sincere prayer that by the end of this book, you feel both equipped and encouraged to walk in your Kingdom Identity. It is our belief that there is a great deal to learn from the 6th chapter of Judges and the story of Gideon.

Chapter 1
Why Your God-sized identity Matters
by Yasha Jones Becton

Prayer

Heavenly Father,

Thank You for Your many blessings towards me. Thank You for all You have done and all that You continue to do in my life. You love me more than my mind is able to comprehend. Father, today, I come to You humbly asking that You show me who I am. As You release and reveal to me who I am, I commit to believe You, to take You at your Word, to trust You, and to follow You even the more. Reveal my identity in such a way that I will be able to walk with clarity, confidence, and conviction from this day forward.

In Jesus Name I pray,

Amen.

When I was in my early twenties, a close friend and I attended a tent revival. The revivalist, may she rest in peace, was known to minister with Holy Ghost boldness and with power. Although I was a college student with one foot in the church and one foot out, I still loved to watch and listen to fiery men and women of God minister the Word of God with signs, wonders, and miracles following. I absolutely loved to hear the preached Word of God which still remains a passion of mine to this day. That night, I was not disappointed!!!

While I cannot tell you what she preached that night, I can tell you the prophetic words she spoke to me personally; were words that would immediately elevate my perspective on my personal walk with Christ and my understanding of the call of God on my life. That night, the woman of God called me an "Evangelist," and she confirmed that I had been called to preach and teach the Word of God. She also told me not to worry about who I would "be like." She assured me that God wanted me to just be myself.

I have to admit that this news was not completely new to me. God had previously spoken to my spirit that He was calling me to be an Evangelist. But I had numerous questions. At the time, I knew nothing about the fivefold ministry gifts (apostle, prophets, pastors, evangelists, and teachers). Further, at the church I attended as a child, there was no such thing as an Evangelist – male or female. Everyone was called a Reverend, Pastor, or a Minister. Why would God call me to be something that was not modeled before me?

Once God spoke this to me, I immediately began my research in the Bible, which started with a study of Philip. Later, I learned that an Evangelist was simply someone called to preach and/or teach the Word of God for the purpose of winning souls to Jesus Christ. I also learned that Evangelists experience tremendous joy when sharing the gospel with people that are hearing it for the first time. That definitely sounded like me. But, why would God call someone like me to preach or teach His Word? And now, this powerful woman of God is confirming that the voice I heard was indeed God. She was confirming that God truly had a divine purpose for my life.

2

After leaving the church I attended as a child, I transitioned to a Pentecostal church. Now, there were Evangelists, Missionaries, Prophets, etc. But they appeared far too holy for someone like me to be included in their ranks. How did the woman of God know I was struggling with the idea of who I would be like? And now God is using her to tell me I can just be myself. Is God sure? Doesn't He know me?

It's now approximately twenty-five years later, and I still remember what was spoken to me. It was on that night that I was properly identified with one of my kingdom assignments. Since that time, I was later licensed as an Evangelist, ordained as a Pastor and later affirmed as a Prophet of God. Yet and still, answering the call to minister the Word of God started one summer night in a tent revival. Not only was I properly identified, but I was released and given the freedom to not be a carbon copy of anyone else, a feeling that continues to remain a tremendous relief. Sometimes I fail at my assignment and some days I miss the mark. But I refuse to miss the mark because I am striving to be like someone else.

Properly Identified

Whether it's for entering public school, transitioning to higher education, boarding a plane, or securing a job, at some point, each of us will have to establish our true identity. We may be asked to present our driver's license, our birth certificate, or a social security card to verify our identity. In some cases, such as high-security jobs, there may even be background checks as well as reference checks. All of this is in an effort to gather as much information as possible pertaining to a person's true identity.

3

Promotions, transitions, and destinations can all be hindered or halted if one is not properly identified.

In this book, *Properly Id'd*, we tackle the topic of identity from a spiritual perspective. We do so with the belief that understanding and embracing our true spiritual identity is a matter of urgency and eternal importance. For the purpose of this book, we will utilize the terms "Kingdom identity," "true identity," and "identity" interchangeably. Here, your *Kingdom identity* is defined as the divine purpose for which you have been created and the unique characteristics (divine makeup) that have been invested in you to equip you to accomplish your Kingdom assignment. To further understand this concept, I invite you to study three key passages of scripture.

Psalm 139:14 (KJV)
I will praise thee; for I am fearfully and wonderfully made: marvelous are thy works; and that my soul knoweth right well.

Jeremiah 18:3-4 (KJV)
Then I went down to the potter's house, and, behold, he wrought a work on the wheels.
And the vessel that he made of clay was marred in the hand of the potter: so he made it again another vessel, as seemed good to the potter to make it.

Jeremiah 1:4-5 (KJV)
Then the word of the LORD came unto me, saying,
Before I formed thee in the belly I knew thee; and before thou camest forth out of the womb, I sanctified thee, and I ordained thee a prophet unto the nations.

Life-Sustaining Principle

…understanding and embracing our true spiritual identity is a matter of urgency and eternal importance.

Each of these scriptural texts illuminates the fact that we were not simply created. God had a masterful plan when He created us, and every aspect of what He created is intentional.

When we examine the life of Jesus, we understand that Jesus had one primary assignment. He was to die on the cross and offer his life as a ransom for many (Matthew 20:28). Jesus completed His assignment and, thankfully, you and I don't have to experience death as the penalty for our sins if we have accepted the finished work of Jesus on the cross. Jesus fulfilled and completed that which was the good and acceptable and perfect will of God for His life (Romans 12:2b). Now, it's our turn. Now, we as workers together with Christ, are called and commissioned to do greater works (2 Corinthians 6:1, John 14:12).

So, the question then becomes, why are you here? What is your Kingdom assignment? Are you walking in your Kingdom identity?

Introducing Jesus Christ

One of the most riveting performances given by the comedian Steve Harvey was the time when he offered an introduction for Jesus Christ. It was simply amazing. Yet, as I ponder it now, it should be easy for a believer to introduce Jesus now because He has so many wonderful miracles recorded in the Bible. And for those that know Him as Saviour and Lord, we can draw from our own personal experiences to provide a proper and fitting introduction. But for the sake of understanding the topic of identity, I want us to examine how Jesus Christ was identified and introduced by the Father. Let's look at one of the Father's official announcements.

When an Announcement Makes it Official

Matthew 3:13-17 (KJV)
Then cometh Jesus from Galilee to Jordan unto John, to be baptized of him. But John forbad him, saying, I have need to be baptized of thee, and comest thou to me? And Jesus answering said unto him, Suffer it to be so now: for thus it becometh us to fulfil all righteousness. Then he suffered him. And Jesus, when he was baptized, went up straightway out of the water: and, lo, the heavens were opened unto him, and he saw the Spirit of God descending like a dove, and lighting upon him: And lo a voice from heaven, saying, This is my beloved Son, in whom I am well pleased.

While Jesus had been identified to Mary and Joseph prior to his birth, here we find an official announcement. Jesus goes to John in order for John to baptize him. John naturally shies away from such a prominent task. After being convinced by Jesus to proceed, we see three things happen. One, the heavens opened up. Secondly, a dove descended upon Jesus. And thirdly, there was a public announcement. A voice from heaven establishes Jesus' identity. This is my beloved Son, in whom I am well pleased.

When we talk about being properly identified, one way that God still identifies us is through a prophetic or spirit-prompted announcement. Here, I will need you to put your spiritual antennas up and listen carefully. When some of us here "announcement" we think theatrics - stage and large audience. The significance of this prophetic announcement is not determined by how loud the person speaks into a microphone or by how large the crowd is that is hearing the declaration. Instead, the significance and the weight of a prophetic announcement rest, not on the size of the audience, but rather on the degree of accuracy to which your Kingdom identity is clearly articulated and subsequently released into the earth realm. As I shared with my own personal story, I knew that God had called me to be an Evangelist. Yet, it wasn't until that assignment was prophetically announced in the Earth (by another person – specifically a Holy Ghost filled believer) that I felt a release (and confirmation) to walk in what God had called me to do.

Life-Sustaining Principle

The significance and the weight of a prophetic announcement rest, not on the size of the audience, but rather on the degree of accuracy to which your Kingdom identity is clearly articulated and subsequently released into the earth realm.

I believe that something breaks in the spirit realm when you are properly identified and announced by prophetically assigned voices. John the Baptist was a prophet. And while I'm not saying that you have to be announced by a prophet, I am saying that the Spirit of God has the authority to sanction someone else to speak prophetically into the atmosphere with clarity and precision about your true identity. This is why it is critical to have spiritual leaders who walk by the spirit so they can see you properly and then call you forth prophetically. Too many believers are being reminded of their past instead of hearing prophetically who they are destined to be. When the spirit of God announces your Kingdom identity in the earth realm, that moment will be marked by elevation, impartation, and validation.

Life-Sustaining Principle

It is critical to have spiritual leaders who walk by the spirit so they can see you properly and then call you forth prophetically.

When we get it right on earth, the results are immediate. When we get it right on earth, heaven backs us up with movement and agreement (Matthew 18:18). When Jesus ascended from the water, after John the Baptist baptized him, the Bible says that the heavens opened up. I believe it symbolized that there was no longer a separation or a barrier between Jesus' heavenly assignment and his earthly agenda. When your heavenly assignment and earthly agenda collide, it automatically creates momentum in the earth. The Father was getting ready to announce and introduce His beloved Son. The announcement would be accompanied by an immediate elevation.

The prophetic announcement of who you are in the earth through an authorized voice sanctions you to walk in your Kingdom identity in the earth. Please understand this, if you were in heaven, no prophetic announcement would be needed concerning your identity, because your identity is not being disputed in heaven. But since you are here on Earth where your spiritual identity can be disputed, dismissed, diminished and attacked, when it is prophetically announced into this earthly atmosphere, it serves as a catalyst to propel you into your destiny. When you are accurately and prophetically announced in this earthly atmosphere, heaven says, "okay, now, let's go to work!"

Life-Sustaining Principle

The prophetic announcement of who you are in the earth through an authorized voice sanctions you to walk in your Kingdom identity in the earth.

Yet, when it comes to our Kingdom assignment, these things are far too glorious for us to accomplish them in and of ourselves. After the heavens opened up, the scripture says that the spirit of God descended like a dove. This represents the impartation. What can we accomplish for our heavenly Father without the impartation of the Holy Spirit? My answer would be absolutely nothing. The Biblical answer is absolutely nothing

(John 15:5). We must be equipped by the Holy Spirit to carry out the assignment or assignments that have been entrusted to us.

Not only did the heavens open up, but God, the Father, offers validation that this is indeed my son. Not just my son, but my beloved son. My beloved son in whom I am well pleased. He validates Jesus in front of the people. He's my son, and I'm well pleased.

Prophetic Announcements Often Followed by Satanic Attacks

Matthew 4:1 (KJV)
Then was Jesus led up of the Spirit into the wilderness to be tempted of the devil.

You should be warned to be careful of chasing or racing to acquire a prophetic announcement. Sometimes, as people, we embark upon an intense search of public validation because we lack the inner assurance and fortitude to stand in our Kingdom Identity. Man-made validations cannot serve to adequately support a God-breathed or God-sized identity. This is why the prophetic announcements around identity must indeed be God-inspired.

Life-Sustaining Principle

Man-made validations cannot serve to adequately support a God-breathed or God-sized identity.

It's also important to note that prophetic announcements are often followed by intense times of testing. Why did the Father have to make it clear that He was well pleased with His son? Take a moment to review Matthew the fourth chapter. Jesus was about to enter into a season of serious testing and temptation. He wanted it to be resolute in the mind and heart of Jesus that the Father takes great pleasure in you. What you are about to experience has little to do with what you've done and everything to do with who you are. Job lost everything he had, not because of a secret sin, but because he was beloved and recommended by the Father. This is also what we must remember when we too enter into great times of testing and temptation. The Father takes great pleasure in you. One of the underlying themes within this book is the importance of every believer understanding that God is for you and not against you.

Identifying, understanding and walking in your God-sized identity automatically qualifies you for a heightened level of spiritual warfare. If you are not operating in purpose and living a life devoid of purpose, there really is no purpose for the enemy to pursue you. Yet, once you step in, or in some cases step near, your God-sized identity and begin to tap into your various Kingdom assignments, you are going to be fought in the Spirit realm. You are going to be tested on new levels. The enemy has a way of showing his hand and revealing himself when you are close to or operating in your purpose. Be "in-couraged," the Father takes great pleasure in you. Don't allow the spiritual warfare to cause you to abandon your Kingdom identity.

Four Pockets – Which Pocket Will You Reach Into?

So, you are holding and reading this book with a very important decision to make. Will you walk in your true Kingdom identity or will you settle for a life that is completely focused on something other than God's divine purpose for your life? As believers, we have one thing to prove. We are challenged to prove what is that good, acceptable, and perfect will of God (Romans 12:2b).

Please make no mistake. Whether you live out your true identity or not, it is all about the choices and decisions you make. When we think of how our Kingdom identity is discovered and further established, we can think of it in this way. Imagine that you are wearing a pair of jeans. The average pair of jeans has at least four pockets, two pockets in the front and usually two pockets in the back. In the pair of jeans that you are wearing, there is money (value) in each pocket. However, each pocket has a different value associated with it. Also, there is one pocket that is filled with a treasure that has unrivaled and unlimited value. Naturally, if you were aware of which pocket housed this treasure, that would be the pocket you would protect and also when in search of something of value, that would be the pocket that you would access. For the sake of this analogy and for the sake of understanding the power of identity, let's explore the four pockets. The four pockets include the popularity pocket, the personality pocket, the pity pocket, and the purpose pocket. In essence, as a believer, you can pull or base your identity on any one of these four areas. Your identity can be based on your popularity, your personality, your level of pity or self-indulgence, or your God-ordained purpose.

Pocket #1 – Popularity Pocket

The first pocket is called the "popularity pocket." The popularity pocket is a front pocket because of its visibility. People that retrieve their identity from the popularity pocket center their actions and behavior around pleasing others. They focus on those things that would positively influence or win the approval of an audience. The popularity pocket is people-situated, meaning the primary aim is to please people and all efforts are focused to that end. Therefore, the value of the "popularity pocket" fluctuates according to the moods and the mindsets of people. You can occasionally reach into the popularity pocket and find something of value, but the popularity pocket will prove to be inconsistent in regard to long-term investments and will prove an impossibility for undergirding your Kingdom purpose or spiritual identity.

Further, the popularity pocket is often a direct threat to godly living and established boundaries. Sometimes popular behavior is synonymous with ungodly and/or unacceptable behavior. Just take a moment to browse any one of our social media outlets. Some people go through great lengths to secure momentary approval from a mass audience. Using your popularity to fuel your spiritual identity is futile and, in some cases, dangerous. As demonstrated in the life of Jesus, sometimes pursuing the will of God for your life will prove anything but popular.

Pocket #2 – Personality Pocket

The personality pocket is also a front pocket. It's equally as visible as the popularity pocket. The personality pocket is "individual" situated, meaning the depth of the pocket is determined by the charisma and depth of the personality of the person. When we meet people, we sense and become aware of that person's personality almost immediately. Do they like to talk? Do they talk too much? Do they enjoy being around people? Do people gravitate to them in a way that is magnetizing? Whether introverted and quiet or extroverted and talkative, we all possess some type of personality.

When your spiritual identity is fueled by your personality, you are blessed by the strengths of your personality, but also limited by the weaknesses associated with your personality. Your Kingdom Identity does not abide in the constraints of your real or perceived weaknesses. Ask Moses.

When God initially called me to be an Evangelist, I was terrified. At the time, I struggled with having day-to-day conversations, and I preferred to communicate in writing. I was not a talker. Talking to people drained me. In my first year of teaching public school, I believe I was in bed before 6 pm because I was so drained from communicating all day.

Life-Sustaining Principle

When your spiritual identity is fueled by your personality, you are blessed by the strengths of your personality, but also limited by the weaknesses associated with your personality.

Fast forward to now, very few people actually believe this to be my testimony because now I speak for a living. If I had allowed my spiritual identity to rest in my personality, I would have never been obedient to the call to preach God's word to any audience. Additionally, my true personality would have served as the ceiling for my Kingdom Assignment. God's call and assignment for our lives operates above and beyond our personalities. The anointing of God supersedes the inhibitions of your personality. Your personality can enhance your Kingdom identity, but it was never intended to house it.

My introverted personality would have said, "no, that's not for me" (in terms of a calling to preach and teach). It would have also said no to pastoring and a few other Kingdom assignments I have received over the last two decades. Instead, the call of God prompted me to surrender (at the time) my greatest weakness to God in expectation of being equipped by the Holy Spirit to fulfill the assignment I had been given. Don't allow your personality to confine your true spiritual identity.

2 Corinthians 12:9 (KJV)
And he said unto me, My grace is sufficient for thee: for my strength is made perfect in weakness. Most gladly therefore will I rather glory in my infirmities, that the power of Christ may rest upon me.

It is also important to note that the opposite is true. Don't allow your personality to overshadow your true spiritual identity. This is especially true for people that have charming extroverted personalities. The church has often confused charisma with character and personality with power. When we understand our true Kingdom identity we cease relying heavily on anything the flesh can produce.

Pocket #3 – Pity Pocket

The third pocket is the pity pocket. The pity pocket is a back pocket – it's designed to take you backwards. Please understand, forward is both a decision and a direction. The pity pocket is a deep pocket, but it contains little to no value. While the popularity pocket is situated around people, and the personality pocket is situated around the individual, the pity pocket is situated around trauma. People that choose to secure their identity from the pity pocket seek to establish their identity around something traumatic or extremely troubling that happened to them or someone close to them. We are not talking about a story of survival, but rather choosing to bathe your identity in a story of trauma. A number of you, like me, have been there when something traumatic happens and it threatens to permanently destroy your progress and redefine your identity. Sometimes one of the most difficult and challenging things to do is to find purpose in tragedy or trauma.

Everything that happens to us is not God-sent or God-orchestrated. Yet, God still promises us in His Word that He will cause all things to work together for our good. He promises to give us beauty for ashes and the oil of joy for mourning (Isaiah 61:3). This lets me know that I don't have to pull my Kingdom identity from a place of trauma or out of the pity pocket. Although there have been times and seasons when I too have been overwhelmed with depression, pity, and utter darkness. Yet, God convinced me that there was hope in my future. And today, I extend that same hope to some of you reading this book. There is hope in your future.

The danger of trying to retrieve anything of value from the pity pocket is the realization that the enemy does not play fair. Satan comes to steal, to kill, and to destroy (John 10:10). I see this as the enemy's progressive agenda. He will steal a moment, then kill a dream, only to ultimately destroy your legacy. Choosing to dwell in pity threatens to hinder the promises and purpose of God from being realized.

Pocket #4 – The Purpose Pocket

In this analogy, the safest and smartest place for a believer to draw his or her identity is from their purpose pocket. The purpose pocket is a back pocket because more often than not, it is hidden from plain sight. The purpose pocket is valuable because it houses God's purpose and plan for your life. What did the potter have in mind when He created you? This is when your identity is not situated in people, not even in your personality, and certainly not in your trauma. This is when your identity is situated in the perfect will of God. When you situate your identity in your divine purpose, you will be able to access the supernatural power of God. Heaven backs you on earth.

In this book, we will use the sixth chapter of Judges, the story of Gideon, and other Biblical scriptures as a backdrop to demonstrate how we become properly id'd or properly identified. Gideon, like many of us, finds himself being given a divine assignment he felt ill-equipped to carry out. Yet, he decides to reach into his purpose pocket. As a result, we are talking about him thousands of years later.

Embracing Your God-sized Identity

This is an urgent matter, and the time is now for you to embrace your God-sized identity. Before we start our journey, here are a few things to keep in mind about your God-sized identity.

1. Your God-sized identity is Jesus-Centered. It is important that you understand our discussion about identity starts, ends and is sustained in Jesus Christ. John 15:5 states, "I am the vine, ye are the branches: He that abideth in me, and I in him, the same bringeth forth much fruit: for without me ye can do nothing." Without Him we can do nothing. Without Him, there is no God-sized identity, just meaningless existence.

2. Remember, there is no dispute in heaven about who you are. If there is any confusion about your identity, it rests solely in this natural realm - here on earth. It is critically important that any identity-related confusion does not find it's resting place in your heart or in your mind.

3. Struggles related to acceptance of your God-sized identity are usually the result of an inaccurate view or understanding of God, an inaccurate view or understanding of ourselves, or a pattern of abuse or neglect in our past that has somewhat distorted our perspective.

4. God-Sized also means that your natural mind may have difficulty understanding an identity that was birthed in heaven. This is why it often requires a shift in the way we think and how we see ourselves.

If you are reading this book and think of yourself as anything less than really important and significant to God, then you do not fully understand your God-sized identity. It's super-sized. It is the complete opposite of small and insignificant. Are you ready to embrace your God-sized identity? Are you ready to be properly id'd?

<u>Questions</u>

1. Can you recall a public or private moment when you were "properly identified" by someone else? Elaborate here.

_____

_____

_____

_____

2. Why is understanding your spiritual identity a matter of urgency? (See Psalm 90:12)

_____

_____

_____

_____

3. What will you commit to doing to delve deeper into your knowledge about your Kingdom assignment(s)?

_____

_____

_____

_____

4. In 21 words or less, based on your life story, write an introduction of Jesus.

_____

_____

_____

_____

5. Have you ever tried to retrieve your identity from the Pity Pocket? What valuable lessons have you learned?

_____

_____

_____

_____

6. How can you commit to only retrieving your identity from the purpose pocket? What are some practical things that you can do to cease relying on your popularity, personality, or pity pocket?

_____

_____

_____

Chapter 2
Released from the Hands of the Thief
by Kristen Baker

Scripture: Judges 6:1-6 KJV

And the children of Israel did evil in the sight of the LORD: and the LORD delivered them into the hand of Midian seven years. ² And the hand of Midian prevailed against Israel: and because of the Midianites the children of Israel made them the dens which are in the mountains, and caves, and strong holds. ³ And so it was, when Israel had sown, that the Midianites came up, and the Amalekites, and the children of the east, even they came up against them; ⁴ And they encamped against them, and destroyed the increase of the earth, till thou come unto Gaza, and left no sustenance for Israel, neither sheep, nor ox, nor ass. ⁵ For they came up with their cattle and their tents, and they came as grasshoppers for multitude; for both they and their camels were without number: and they entered into the land to destroy it. ⁶ And Israel was greatly impoverished because of the Midianites; and the children of Israel cried unto the LORD.

Prayer

Father,

As we continue this journey to being properly identified, we ask that You give us courage and boldness to commit to and finish the process. I am confident that what You have started You will complete. Expose any iniquity or sin that must be dealt with in order to provide a fresh canvas for You to create in me what You ordained from the beginning of time. I relinquish my plan, my timeline, my desires in exchange for Yours because You know all things, and You know what's best for me.

In Jesus name,
Amen.

Greatness through your God-ordained identity is within your immediate reach, once you have been released from the hands of the thief. John 10:10 (NKJV) states, "The thief does not come except to steal, and to kill, and to destroy. I have come that they may have life, and that they may have *it* more abundantly." The thief is Satan himself. He comes to steal what is not his to take, kill what is not his to end (or crucify), and destroy what is not his to damage. Satan is cunning and shrewd. He often cannot physically steal, kill, or destroy us, so he uses his power to do it both spiritually and emotionally. Satan has an all-out play to kill your passion, steal your joy, and destroy both your destiny and your witness. He would love to see you serve the all-powerful God and lack power. He would love to see you serve the all-knowing God and be lost. He would love for you to have a loving Father and not feel loved or full of life. We must protect what God has given us.

One of Satan aliases is the prince of the power of the air (Ephesians 2:2). I used to wonder why he had any authority over anything. It bothered me for so long until I realized that a prince only has the power that the King gives him. His power is limited, but one of the ways he operates is if we give him access. Many times in life, we leave "gates" open for Satan to gain access. Gates are associated with our senses. Our eyes, ears, mouths, noses, and hands are representative of our gates. For example, it is important that we monitor what we hear and listen to because our ears are a gateway to the soul. Like any thief, all he needs is a foothold. It is important to understand that without God, man can do nothing, and without man, God will do nothing. We must be in partnership with God to thrive. Why is this important? I'm glad you asked. As children of God, Satan only has the power in our lives that we allow him to have. Therefore, we must walk in the power God has given us. He told us through Adam to "Be fruitful, and multiply, and replenish the earth, and subdue it: and have dominion..." (Genesis 1:28 KJV). When we walk in our God-sized identity and God-given authority, we strip the thief of his power to end what God has already started. Be confident that what God started, you will see it completed.

Life-Sustaining Principle

It is important to understand that without God, man can do nothing, and without man, God will do nothing.

Preparing to Be Properly Identified

As previously stated, it is only a creator that knows the true purpose and essence of its creation. God is our Father and Creator and knows why and for what purpose He created us. Genesis tells us that we were made in the image and likeness of God; our identity is in Him. We are because He is. From the foundation of the earth, we were like God. Before we were even an image on a sonogram, we were like our Heavenly Father. We were destined to have dominion, authority, and power in the earth. He formed a covenant, a contractual agreement, with Israel that He would be their God and they His people. It was not until sin entered into the world that we strayed away from God's original intent and broke the agreement. It was with one man's disobedience that sin entered into the world and by one Man's obedience that nothing, including sin, would separate us from God's love.

The Interruption of Sin

In Genesis 2, after God made Adam and Eve, He gave them permission to eat of any tree of their choice except for the tree of knowledge of good and evil. It was the consumption of this tree that caused their eyes to be opened. Prior to this text in chapter 2 notice that everything God made was good. God called the dry land Earth and gathered together the waters and called the seas: and God saw that is was *good (vs. 10)*. And the earth brought forth grass and herb yielding seed after his kind, and the tree yielding fruit, whose seed was in itself, after his kind: and God saw that it was *good (vs. 12)*. And God set them in the firmament of the heaven to give light upon the earth, And to rule over the day and over the night, and to divide the light from the darkness: and God saw that it was *good (vs. 17-18)*. The scripture continues on to show that everything God made was good but He, again, did not want them or rather forbade them from eating of this particular tree.

It is interesting to me that it was not the tree of good and evil, but the tree of knowledge of good and evil. This is significant to me because it speaks to the character of a Father, Abba. Here both Adam and Eve have only known what was good, yet, here God is trying to help protect their innocence and communion with Him. I believe that God was trying to keep them from the knowledge of an experience of evil when they, up until this point, knew no evil.

While the Bible does not explicitly say that Adam and Eve agreed to abstain from the tree of knowledge of good and evil, I believe that we can assume they agreed because they walked with God and were in constant fellowship with Him. Their only desire was to please Him. Consequently, they must have agreed to God's one request. Adam and Eve's sin not only opened their eyes to what they had yet to see, but it also broke the fellowship they once had with the Father and caused death. While at the moment Adam and Eve did not die physically (even though that was a consequence that was to come), they died spiritually. Sin separates us from God. God is life. To be separated from life is surely death, both spiritually and even emotionally. In the Old Testament an offering, typically a lamb or bullock, had to be sacrificed as recompense for sin. It could not be just any animal. To atone or appease, it must be a perfect sacrifice to make amends for the sin. Jesus was that perfect lamb. He is the Word wrapped in flesh.

Every prophecy, epistle, piece of poetry, and every single word of the Bible points to God reconciling His children back to Himself. We see all throughout the Word of God, how Israel goes in and out of covenant with God. If we would be honest, we must admit that like Israel, the chosen ones, we sometimes find ourselves drifting away from God, the source of our true identity. We see in Judges chapter 6 verse one, the Israelites did evil in the eyes of the LORD *again,* and for seven years, He gave them into the hands of the Midianites.

A Father Committed to Completion

There are several observations we find in this text. But first, how significant is it that Israel was oppressed for seven years? We often hear of the spiritual significance of the number seven and see the number quite often in the Bible. For example, Noah was instructed to take seven pairs of animals into the ark. Jacob worked seven years (twice) to marry Rachel (Gen 29:18-30). Naaman was dipped seven times in the Jordan for recovery of his sight (2Kings 5). In the book of Revelation alone, there are seven seals, seven letters to the seven churches, and seven angels with seven trumpets. We could go on and on, but seven is the number of completion and totality. To take it a step further, the number seven denotes the completion of a divine mandate - divine perfection. Why is this even important? I believe that this is significant when we are reaping the harvest of sin. Galatians 6:7-8 (NLT) reminds us… "Don't be misled—you cannot mock the justice of God. You will always harvest what you plant. Those who live only to satisfy their own sinful nature will harvest decay and death from that sinful nature. But those who live to please the Spirit will harvest everlasting life from the Spirit." According to the Word of God (Galatians 6:8), if we sow to the flesh, we will reap of the flesh, and the same is true if we sow in the spirit. As long as the earth remains, there will be seedtime and harvest (Gen 8:22). I believe that this is an important reminder that everything we do and say is a seed. It is up to us to make sure that the seeds we sow are sown to the spirit and not to the flesh.

Life-Sustaining Principle

... this is an important reminder that everything we do and say is a seed. It is up to us to make sure that the seeds we sow are sown to the spirit and not to the flesh.

I can remember, before I fully submitted my life to God, sowing seeds of deception and rejection. Years later, I became the grantee of the very things I was once the grantor. I began to experience the very things I had done to other people. But, I can certainly rejoice in everything I endured! I rejoiced not only because I kept going long enough to see all those things work out for good. I can also rejoice in knowing that what I received was less than what I deserved! I rejoice in knowing that what God started in me He is continuously completing. It should be our prayer that God completes His work within us. I am not saying you will endure your hardship for seven years. For some, it maybe three months, others a year, for others several years. What I am saying is that we must allow God to complete what He is doing in us. I believe that as we go through, whether self-inflicted or God-ordained, He often wants to build us in three areas: patience, perfection, and prayer.

The Perfect Work of Patience

I ask God questions often. I began to think of the many instances in the Bible where words such as straightway, suddenly, immediately, speedily, quickly, etc. are used. I asked myself, "if we serve a God who can do anything and everything instantly (and He can), why would He want us to be patient?" In a world of microwaves, smartphones, and pre-cooked meals, it is no wonder we are spoiled by concepts that get us what we want when we want it and how we want it. I am guilty of ordering food from my favorite restaurant while I am on the way there so when I get there, I can run inside, grab it and go, or go through the drive-thru without even having to get out of my car. While there are some things in life that are okay "on-the-go" many times with the things of God, we must wait.

Why do I have to wait for what you can snap your fingers and accomplish? I mean, come on God! What the Lord said to me was that impatience in life sometimes leads to shortcuts. Shortcuts are options we come up within our own limited strength and intelligence. Shortcuts are often a byproduct of pride. Many times, we minimize the sin called pride. Proverbs 29:23 (KJV) states, "A man's pride shall bring him low: but honour shall uphold the humble in spirit." Pride causes us to feel as if we legitimately are smarter, more powerful, and know more than God. Pride is in operation when we feel as though we need to help God out and

28

create options that He did not give us. When David slept with Bathsheba, he needed a quick way to fix his mistake, so He had Uriah killed. Pride was thinking he could take matters into his own hands and fix one sin with another. Instead of Abraham waiting on God, he took the matter into his own hands and gave birth to a plausible solution but not the promised son. Impatience and pride will often cause you to move out of God's will and His timing. If we were that smart, we would not need Him in the first place. But we need Him every second of the day, whether we realize it or not.

Life-Sustaining Principle

What the Lord said to me was that impatience in life sometimes leads to shortcuts. Shortcuts are options we come up within our own limited strength and intelligence. Shortcuts are often a byproduct of pride.

The Work of Perfection

Now, let's look at perfection, not in the sense of being without flaw or fault, but perfection in the sense of maturity. Though it should be the goal, just because we get older, it does not necessarily mean we get better or wiser. Unfortunately, with age, maturity is sold separately. Spiritual maturity is so important. God is a good father. A good parent cares enough about their children to refrain from giving them anything they are not prepared to handle. God often uses the things we go through to mature us. Spiritual maturity, to me, is simply becoming more and more like Him. The more I think, speak, and do what He does, the more perfect I become. We must allow God to complete what He has started in us. It would almost be a waste of time and a waste of God's grace if we go through various tests and trials and never learn or grow from them. Can you imagine getting to the judgment day after all the trials, death, disappointments, storms, and tests in your life only to find that you still missed Heaven? Even when we are to endure the consequences of our sin, we must pray that God completes in us what will make us better and cause Him to be pleased with our life and service. We are blessed in the fact that Jesus paid the price on the cross for the sin of the entire world. Why is this a blessing? It is a blessing because, while we must bear the consequence, we could never bear the price. God so graciously paid a debt He did not owe!

What is also significant about Judges 6:1-7, is that Israel was given into the hands of the Midianites. God will sometimes allow us to experience defeat without Him in order to appreciate victory with Him. I say with "without Him" because essentially the Israelites were living in the sin of disobedience and idolatry. As I previously stated, sin separates us from God. God allowed who they once defeated, Midian, to now be their oppressor (Numbers 31).

Numbers 31:1-12 (KJV)
The Lord said to Moses, "Take vengeance on the Midianites for the Israelites. After that, you will be gathered to your people." So Moses said to the people, "Arm some of your men to go to war against the Midianites so that they may carry out the Lord's vengeance on them. Send into battle a thousand men from each of the tribes of Israel." So twelve thousand men armed for battle, a thousand from each tribe, were supplied from the clans of

Israel. Moses sent them into battle, a thousand from each tribe, along with Phinehas son of Eleazar, the priest, who took with him articles from the sanctuary and the trumpets for signaling. They fought against Midian, as the Lord commanded Moses, and killed every man. Among their victims were Evi, Rekem, Zur, Hur and Reba—the five kings of Midian. They also killed Balaam son of Beor with the sword. The Israelites captured the Midianite women and children and took all the Midianite herds, flocks and goods as plunder. They burned all the towns where the Midianites had settled, as well as all their camps. They took all the plunder and spoils, including the people and animals, and brought the captives, spoils and plunder to Moses and Eleazar the priest and the Israelite assembly at their camp on the plains of Moab, by the Jordan across from Jericho.

Numbers 31 provides a detailed delineation of victory as a result of obedience. The nation was victorious in this battle because they were in right standing with God. When you are totally dependent on God, every success is in His hands. Again, Israel's relationship with God was no ordinary relationship. It was covenantal meaning that God had an obligation (because of His word) to Israel and Israel to God. According to Deuteronomy 28, God gave His people a list of "ultimatums"....if/then statements, if you will. God declared that if my people fully obey Me and follow my commands, I will set you above all nations, I will bless you in the city and in the field, I will bless the fruit of your wombs, I will bless your land and your crops, I will bring victory over your enemies and so many other promises. We see that because Israel broke the covenant, the opposite happened to them for seven years.

The Perfect Work of Prayer

The third and final area of perfection is prayer. Prayer is essential in the life of the believer. It is consistent communication with God that heightens our ears to God's voice of direction. However, if we are to be properly Id'd, it is not enough to pray to God. Yes, you read it correctly. We cannot afford to only pray *to* God, but we must learn to pray *with* God. Hebrews 7:25 reminds us that He ever lives to make intercession for us. If God is forever praying on behalf of His people, shouldn't we be praying with Him? After all, He knows everything. The inheritance of the saints is that we can come boldly before the throne of grace in prayer, but we must learn to tap into the river of intercession. If we are not careful, we can get into the habit of praying from our limited knowledge and limitless emotions. However, if we are to walk confidently in our true identity as the children of God, we must pray according to His will. It is when we achieve this that He responds.

The Benefit of Hardship Under His Hand

Even as we suffer the consequences of our disobedience, there is a reason to give God thanks! We can rejoice in the fact that even our punishment is less than what we really deserve. God promised that after we have suffered a while, He would settle, strengthen, establish, and perfect us- divine perfection (1 Peter 5:10).

There is more good news in the simple fact that God's glory is revealed even in our oppression. We see the grace, mercy, and love of God even in the fact that He allows us to go through it, but if we repent and turn to Him, we are never destroyed by it.

Avoiding Caves

Judges 6:2 Because the power of Midian was so oppressive, the Israelites prepared shelters for themselves in mountain clefts, caves, and strongholds.

The vehicle of sin has a way of not only driving you away from God but into "caves" (Judges 6:2 KJV). Caves of insecurity. Caves of fear. Caves of self-consciousness. Caves of depression. Caves of mistaken identity. Disobedience to the call of God will cause you to make a place fit that was never meant for habitation. How many times do we waste energy on forcing what does not fit instead of using that energy towards our obedience to God? Check your energy level and take a hard look at what you may be spending effort on that is outside of your divine purpose; God's reason for creating you to be uniquely you. Don't get me wrong. It is so easy to get caught up in what is around us that we lose sight of, what Paul called, weightier matters. God's will and our obedience must be a priority in our lives. He must always be the object of our focus.

Life-Sustaining Principle

The vehicle of sin has a way of not only driving you away from God but into "caves" (Judges 6:2 KJV) … Disobedience to the call of God will cause you to make a place fit that was never meant for habitation.

Believe it or not, focus is inevitable. There is no shortage of things for our minds to focus on. We often focus on our families; we may focus on our problems and even the world around us. However, there must be intention around making God our focus and the object of our worship and study. As we begin to embark upon this study, my prayer is that God will not only open our eyes but that He will reveal more and more of our identity. We can see from the Israelites' example in Judges 6:1-5 that God pours revelation on those who are in a posture to receive. That posture is one of obedience. God gives revelation to those who walk in willful obedience to His commands.

I want to close this chapter with two appeals. The first appeal is to youth and young adults. Here's my quick question, "Do you want to be free?" Understand, you can't divorce anything you want to stay married to. Remove yourself from relationships and environments that give the old you a place of comfort. To the church, understand that the younger generation needs your testimonies. Most people that are in sin do not need help with feeling guilty; they already are. We, the church, must offer them what they need first and foremost...love. We can do this by eliminating judgment and increasing grace. Once we have built a relationship, then we can address behavior. Addressing behavior before youth or young adults feel like they belong, often yields unfruitful results.

Questions

1. What are some ways you are impatient? In what ways could that lead to you creating your own shortcut and operating in pride?

_____

_____

_____

_____

2. How are you going through in an area and what do you think God may be trying to complete in you?

_____

_____

_____

_____

3. What is at least one practical way that you can start to pray with God and not just to God?

_____

_____

_____

_____

4. What "caves" have you made livable in your life?

_____

_____

_____

_____

5. What are things you can do to increase your focus on the things of God?

_____

_____

_____

_____

6. Make a list of what you feel are the priorities in your life. Remain prayerful. As situations arise that do not fit in any category, make a conscious effort to refrain from such things (unless otherwise instructed by the Lord). Stay focused.

_____

_____

_____

_____

Chapter 3

Receiving Prophetic Correction and Divine Impartation
by Gert Thompson

Scripture: Judges 6:7-10

> [7] And it came to pass, when the children of Israel cried unto the LORD because of the Midianites,
> [8] That the LORD sent a prophet unto the children of Israel, which said unto them, Thus saith the LORD God of Israel, I brought you up from Egypt, and brought you forth out of the house of bondage; [9] And I delivered you out of the hand of the Egyptians, and out of the hand of all that oppressed you, and drave them out from before you, and gave you their land; [10] And I said unto you, I am the LORD your God; fear not the gods of the Amorites, in whose land ye dwell: but ye have not obeyed my voice.

Prayer

To the greatest Prophet that ever lived, our most High God and Almighty King. We know you to be the God of prophetic correction and divine impartation; we say thank You. Our hearts are thankful because we get to be employed for service and deployed into regions, countries, and nations to impart prophetically into those we divinely encounter. For our generation, the younger generations and those yet to be born, thank You for choosing us to leave a wealthy spiritual legacy that You will be glorified through your Son, Jesus the Christ.

May the message of this chapter massage the hearts of those who read it with openness and receptivity. May the call to answer You be obeyed and the will for total surrender be accomplished by the powerful name of Jesus as we bring glory to Your name.

Amen!

Openness is a necessary criterion for receiving anything. When the thing received is good to you, it feels good to you, or makes life easier for you, it's easy to receive. On the other hand, correction seems to be difficult to receive when it requires a change from what is familiar and stretches you out of your comfort zone. However, enlarging your spiritual capacity for a kingdom assignment and promotion is always beneficial for growth. You have been filled with the Spirit for more than missing a trip to hell or relaxing on a hammock in the cool breeze.

We ask God to enlarge our territory, but if we are not performing maintenance to the space we have, then there is no need for more. So now we have stunted and stagnated our spiritual capacity. What will you do with more? It is not "more" for "store."

Life-Sustaining Principle

Enlarging your **spiritual capacity** for a kingdom assignment and promotion is always beneficial for growth.

When the birth canal does not have the capacity to birth the baby normally, the mother is assisted by C-section to enlarge her capacity to birth the child. As we prepare for our divine or Kingdom assignment, oftentimes, we have to embrace a similar experience. There will be times you must experience spiritual surgery to enlarge your spiritual capacity for Kingdom assignment. Honestly, the only way I know that you can fully cooperate with God is to be cut, pruned, clipped, challenged and changed for an enlargement of spiritual capacity. John 15 verses 1-2 (KJV) states, "I am the true vine, and my Father is the husbandman. Every branch in me that beareth not fruit he taketh away: and every branch that beareth fruit, he purgeth it, that it may bring forth more fruit." Are you strong enough for the surgery? Are you willing to have the surgery? How does your lab work look?

Life-Sustaining Principle

There will be times you must experience spiritual surgery to enlarge your spiritual capacity for kingdom assignment. Honestly, the only way I know that you can fully cooperate with God is to be cut, pruned, clipped, challenged, and changed.

Change. Change refuses to make peace with the status quo. Change builds a bridge named after itself that becomes the gap (**bridges the gap)** between what is and what could be. Prophetic correction, when properly received, leads to and births change.

When God called me and promoted me to pastoral ministry, I was livid. Yes, I was!! It was not on my to-do-list for life, neither on my bucket list of things I wished to experience before the end of my life. After all, it was "my" life, and I had intelligent plans already lined up for my future. For many readers, this may be your story too, or very close to it.

Life-Sustaining Principle

Change refuses to make peace with the status quo. Prophetic correction, when properly received leads to, and births change.

When God Speaks the Final Word Regarding "Who You Are"

Lesson learned: Six human prophecies were given to me about pastoring, none of which I received. God, himself, was the seventh. As we have learned, seven is the number of completion, spiritual perfection. "And on the seventh day, God ended his work which he had made; and he rested on the seventh day from all His work which He had made. And God blessed the seventh day and sanctified it: because that in it he had rested from all his work which God created and made" (Genesis 2:2-3 KJV). By the seventh prophecy, I stepped into the Kingdom Assignment that is now my everyday reality.

The Seventh Prophecy

With the seventh prophecy, God ended His work of prophecy to me concerning my call to the pastorate. He rested from using all the other vessels He chose to inform me. God brought a powerful, resounding end to that prophetic process. **The Prophet of all prophets prophesied to me one last time**. He blessed that seventh time in a way that clarified to me the seriousness of every prior prophecy.

After all of the human prophecies given to me, God took me to the backside of the desert, just Him and me. "Gert, *tradition* is not talking to you, I Am!!! It's not your life as in the shallow way you think it is. I have the receipt for your life in my scars, on my brow, my side, my feet, and wrists. You are not your own. You have not chosen Me, I chose you from the foundation of the world and if you don't do what I have called you to do - just know that NOTHING else in your life will be successful." As the saying goes, I found myself stuck between a rock and a hard place, while my spirit man was waiting to exhale with "free will". What do you think I did?

I had been cut, bruised, broken, pained, disappointed, had my life changed and rearranged, and brought to tears with a surrendered spirit. I came out with both hands up for a job I didn't even sign up for, wasn't interviewed for, neither promised a paycheck after giving up the paycheck God told me to release. Wow! I must have been crazy or had crazy faith I didn't know I had. After seventeen years of pastoring, I am still in the changing process; it's never-ending.

When it comes to prophetic words, I didn't have to know His choice of vessels, and they didn't need to know me. I should have been counting the number of times I heard the same word and how I repeatedly rejected it. At the seventh prophecy, God indicated that He had set me aside, ordained, and consecrated me for pastoral purposes. The seventh time brought awareness that all my life I had been withheld from ordinary use because I was reserved exclusively for God. This was an uncommon way to make known to me the call on my life. Obviously, God and I were not on the same page, much to my dismay.

Naaman had to go dip seven times in Jordan against his will. He preferred one of the better bodies of water in Damascus in which to immerse himself. As recorded in Second Kings 5:10 (KJV), "And Elisha sent a messenger unto him saying, Go wash in Jordan seven times, and thy flesh shall come again unto thee, and thou shalt be clean." Why do I have to go to Jordan anyway and why do I have to wash seven times? Can't this prophet just approach me, wave his hand over the place of my infirmity and recover the leprosy? Seldom does God ask us to do that which we would easily volunteer. Finally, Naaman submitted, went to Jordan, and came up clean the seventh time.

Joshua and the children of Israel marched around the wall of Jericho, but it didn't fall down until the seventh time on the seventh day. It was on that day, with seven priests and seven trumpets of rams' horns (Joshua 6:4 KJV), that the people shouted at Joshua's command... "So the people shouted when the priests blew with the trumpets: and it came to pass, when the people heard the sound of the trumpet, and the people shouted with a great shout, that the wall fell down flat, so that the people went up into the city, every man straight before him, and they took the city" (Joshua 6:20 KJV).

I don't know if any of the six persons that God sent to me had the gift of prophecy, yet they gave me a prophetic word from God. As believers, we must LEARN to receive the prophetic word of God no matter who God chooses to deliver it through. One day God might decide to promote you to the Office of Prophet or use you to give a prophetic word. I'm sure you would like to be received. Do unto others as you would have them do unto you and that "others" includes God Himself.

Don't do as I did. I had to repent. God waited patiently on me and has favored me to serve in pastoral ministry for the last seventeen years. Where would I be if He had left me in my stupor? All glory and honor are to His name!

Overcoming Self-Made Stupors

In our day-to-day living, there are seasons when we are insensitive to the voice of God, yet we function in our daily work assignments with complete sensitivity. Yes, I'm referring to the work assignments when we check our bank accounts to be sure our paycheck arrived with no unexpected deductions. We act as if we are near unconsciousness when it comes to the work assignments for the Kingdom. There is no mental spontaneity. Therefore, the barely responsive mind cannot generate an energetic body to serve with a Kingdom mindset. This is when you are in a self-made stupor.

When we refuse to engage our mind in something that demands the engagement of the body, we release the spirit of slothfulness to overwhelm our energy pack. We find ourselves stuck in a stupor we allowed to take place. Then we play the blame card. We must engage our minds on the divine exhortations extended to us. Philippians 4:8 NIV Study Bible states, "Finally, brothers, whatever is true, whatever is noble, whatever is right, whatever is pure, whatever is lovely, whatever admirable—if anything is excellent or praiseworthy—think about such things." These are the kinds of thoughts that will energize our thinking which can then serve as energy to our body, which empowers us to serve with a Kingdom mindset.

Choosing to Submit to God's Plan

God's plan comes with provisions that are not always comfortable, visible, or believed to be readily available to you. You cannot avoid the call of God and replace it by abiding in your personal comfort zone expecting that level of comfort to be your companion during the consequences of your compromise. There are consequences to choosing comfort and/or compromise. Remember, He doesn't live in time. He lives in eternity, yet He delivers everything in time on time from eternity. We must learn to trust His eternal timing in our earthly timing. I am still challenged with this at times.

Our entire life is already planned in the mind of God. There is a delivery date on each blessing, event, promotion, impartation, correction, spiritual development, graduation date, and the list goes on. A day with God is as a thousand years, and a thousand years is as a day. Also, God does not wear the Timex watch that was made in time. Once I learned those two things, I stopped stressing myself about when God was going to deliver, manifest, and make good on His promises to me based on the truth of His Word. My focus changed to "me"! I began working on making good my word to God on a consistent basis, not wimping out in weak moments but pulling on the strength of God in those times for continuity in my relationship with Him.

Life-Sustaining Principle

You cannot avoid the call of God and replace it by abiding in your personal comfort zone expecting that level of comfort to be your companion during the consequences of your compromise.

The Necessity of Prophetic Correction

In the sixth chapter of Judges, the children of Israel, of whom Gideon was included, were now in their Promised Land and they seemingly had forgotten about their God and their deliverance from the land of Egypt. They engaged in evil with their enemy right in God's face. Their unethical, immoral behavior and disobedience caused God displeasure. Their enemy turned on them, took everything from them, and came to utterly annihilate them. It took this *magnitude of punishment* to get Israel in a place to cry out to God for help.

As noted in Chapter 1, the Israelites were given into the hands of the Midianites because of their blatant disobedience and disrespect to their God. After the exodus, they became friends with people who were to be removed from the land God promised them.

Instead, they became friends with their enemies, the Midianites. Never trust the kindest deeds from your enemy. The Midianites hooked up with Balak the king of Moab and conspired against the Israelites. The plot was to employ Balaam, a diviner to make an attempt to manipulate God to curse the Israelites, rather than bless them. The reason they desired to curse Israel was so Israel would become weakened and easy to defeat in a battle. Then they would be able to drive them out of the land. Of course, that plan failed because it was the covenanted will of God to bless Israel with the land. Every time Balaam tried to curse Israel, he could only bless them because it was according to God's will. Devils devise devious plans, and so it was with Balaam. He seduced the Israelite soldiers with Larz, the demon of sexual lust via the Moabite women. While staying at Shittim, the soldiers began to indulge in sexual immorality with these women who invited them to the sacrifices to their gods. These men ate the sacrificial meal, bowed down before these gods, and yoked themselves to Baal of Peor. The God of Israel was heated with anger against Israel. Vengeance is Mine, and recompense, in the time when their foot shall slide: for the day of their disaster is at hand, and their doom comes speedily (Deuteronomy 32:35 AMP). It is a fearful (formidable and terrible) thing to incur divine penalties and be cast into the hands of the living God (Hebrews 10:31 AMP). God sent a plague where 24,000 died because of sexual immorality. Phinehas, Aaron's nephew, drove a spear through an Israelite's back and a Moabite woman's stomach. These same Midianites who seduced the Israelites are now being used during Gideon's time to chastise the Israelites for their idolatrous behavior. For you shall worship no other god; for the Lord, Whose name is Jealous, is a jealous (impassioned) God, (Exodus 34:14). Be present wherever you are. Your present will become your history so learn presently for your history's sake, for your history will be useful in your future which will someday become your present. Israel failed this test; they did not learn that God was not going to tolerate their spiritual adultery.

The Israelites were hard workers, trained in Egypt, so when they planted, it was plentiful. When they raised cattle, it was plentiful. God blessed the work of their hands, but the work of their hands did not bless them in return. Instead, their enemies ruined their crops like an army of locusts and did not spare a living thing for Israel, neither sheep, cattle, or donkey. They became so impoverished that they cried out to God for HELP! Seven years of cruel oppression by the Midianites was the lot of the Israelites for their disobedience to God. The easiest way to remain in God's good graces is to repent, humble yourself, seek the face of God and turn from your wicked ways, and He will hear from heaven and heal your land.

What God has for you is for you, but you might have to suffer shipwreck to get it. Even when you have been disobedient, no weapon formed against you shall prosper if it's God's will for you to succeed. Obedience does not exempt you from suffering on the way to your purposed destiny. Obedience to God is terribly important!

Enduring Hardships

God knew the way I would take!! Had I clearly known He was calling me to share the gift of pastoring with the Body of Christ before He called my husband home, dismissed me from

47

employment, and sent me back to school, I would have made every effort to leave the state of South Carolina. Like Abraham, I would have been on my way to "I know not where." The key difference here is that I would have been leading myself rather than allowing God to control my life. So, starting with the dearest to me, He took away the promised husband He had given me. He then told me to give up the least fulfilling thing in my life, which was my job, and sent me to school. This had to be the way to get me fully submitted and committed to pursuing my kingdom prosperity and purposed destiny. The reverential fear of God got my undivided listening attention. He'll get you there one way or another. Yes, at the time, I felt as if God had punished me severely, but it was my unwillingness to cooperate with Him that ushered me into this stupor. I still feel the remorseful pain of my attitude. Yet, He has shown Himself awesomely faithful to me!

The Cry of God's People

God heard the cry of His people and sent a prophet, an authorized spokesman, to remind them of their exodus from Egypt, their relief from oppression and the fact that He gave them a land which did not belong to them originally. They were reminded of who their God was, yet they disobeyed Him. Gideon hears this, and he is in hiding. If Israel is to be saved from the hand of their enemy, someone has to step up to the leadership position.

A Corrected Perception for a New Assignment

Gideon, like me (and some of you), had not applied for the position of leadership. God chose him. The call of God was on his life and this was the time for him to come to the front of the line and respond. He is now in the promoted position of a Front-Line Responder, and he must respond as such! God is doing something new in Gideon before doing something new through him.

Gideon feels inadequate, insecure, and ill-equipped. His mindset and his perception needed correction to establish him with faith in his God to complete this new assignment. He had to confront his doubts and fears within. He finds himself in a closed place with a familiar feeling much like the bondage of his past. This time he is cowering hoping his hiding place will not be discovered. Gideon is afraid to face his enemies. His facial expression and his body language will signify that he can easily be defeated. What is his family going to think of him? They depend on him for provisions, but right about now Gideon needs God's provisions to destroy his enemies so his people can live in peace. Oh, but God knows exactly where you are hiding, and He will come to pull you out because duty calls for your presence and response, front and center. The people's provisions are on the outside of the threshing floor in the enemy's camp.

Gideon is in a closed place threshing wheat where grapes are to be pressed. His wheat is limited. Had the angel not come, had the Midianites not found him, how long did he think he would survive off of raw wheat in the winepress? If he ever left the winepress without divine impartation from God, he would not have survived.

The Necessity of Divine Impartation

The angel comes and sits under an oak watching Gideon. The angel made himself visible to Gideon and began the process of communication. No matter what you think of yourself, be it too high or too low, when God is ready to confront you about the purpose He intentionally created you for, He will confirm that purpose. He alone chooses the vehicle of impartation, the place, and the time. A supernatural inspiration invades your natural norm with a divine infilling of knowledge that overtakes your natural ability to receive with clarity. Beyond a shadow of a doubt, you know you have just met with God on a level above the level you have been living on daily; not necessarily because you have been living improperly, but because He is untraceable. Not even your Google watch, as proficient as it is, can track Him. With the purity of clarity, He confronts, communicates, and confirms your calling with divine impartation and revelation. The angel declares him to be a mighty man of valor. Gideon is not alone. His God is with him. The angel, as a representative of a divine God, brings a divine impartation for Gideon. He listens and receives this divine impartation.

Life-Sustaining Principle

No matter what you think of yourself, be it too high or too low, when God is ready to confront you about the purpose He intentionally created you for, He will confirm that purpose. He alone chooses the vehicle of impartation, the place, and the time.

Affirmation

Within divine impartation, there is affirmation. Gideon was affirmed as a man of strength, no matter what he had been thinking about himself earlier. Valor means strength, army, wealth, might, power, and ability. God grants him conquering power over the Midianites. Gideon had intentions of fighting against flesh and blood, but God had another plan. There were no swords or daggers for Gideon's army, no shields, no bows and arrows, no horses. Gideon had the Sword of the Spirit, which is the word of the God divinely imparted into him as the greatest weapon of all to win this war. Gideon had to be strong in his faith because, in visual reality, those trumpets, pitchers, and lamps looked pretty pathetic up against an army equipped to take them out. Can you imagine their enemy strategizing for the kill and how they will annihilate the Israelites? God did not give Gideon the spirit of fear; neither did He give it to you. Your fear fears you. Arise Gideon get down from your post and conquer this host of Midianites. God gives us the victory if we fight!

Life-Sustaining Principle

Your fear fears you!

Questions

1. Is God trying to enlarge your spiritual capacity and are you open to His plan for enlargement?

_____

_____

_____

_____

2. Are there any divine assignments you feel inadequately prepared to pursue?

_____

_____

_____

_____

3 Are you currently "shelving" any gifts and talents that need to be serving others?

_____

_____

_____

_____

4. Is there a prophetic word you have repeatedly rejected? Why?

_____

_____

_____

_____

5. Have you ever experienced a self-made stupor? Please explain.

_____

_____

_____

_____

6. What are some steps you (or someone else) can take to avoid a state of stupor?

_____

_____

_____

_____

_____

7. How do you foster urgency and faithfulness to God-given Kingdom assignments?

_____

_____

_____

_____

8. Why is it so important to know how the voice of God sounds to you?

_____

_____

_____

_____

_____

9. What is the last spiritual directive you received from
    God?_____

    _____

    _____

    _____

    _____

Chapter 4

Leaving the Wine Press: Discovering Who You Are
by Kylie McBride

Scripture: Judges 6:11-15 KJV

> [11] And there came an angel of the LORD, and sat under an oak which was in Ophrah, that pertained unto Joash the Abiezrite: and his son Gideon threshed wheat by the winepress, to hide it from the Midianites. [12] And the angel of the LORD appeared unto him, and said unto him, The LORD is with thee, thou mighty man of valour. [13] And Gideon said unto him, Oh my Lord, if the LORD be with us, why then is all this befallen us? and where be all his miracles which our fathers told us of, saying, Did not the LORD bring us up from Egypt? but now the LORD hath forsaken us, and delivered us into the hands of the Midianites. [14] And the LORD looked upon him, and said, Go in this thy might, and thou shalt save Israel from the hand of the Midianites: have not I sent thee? [15] And he said unto him, Oh my Lord, wherewith shall I save Israel? behold, my family is poor in Manasseh, and I am the least in my father's house.

Prayer

As the world seeks to define my identity, God, I look to You for clarity about who I am and what You have created me to do. My deepest desire is to manifest Your will for me in my every day, "walking-around life."

There is, in fact, no other way for me to live. Yet, there is a disconnect between this desire and my reality. So often, I find myself in doubt like Gideon. I have read Your promises as outlined by Your Word. I have received the Word of God as it has been spoken into my hearing and settled in my heart. I try my best to simply believe. Yet, I so often find myself hiding and afraid in the winepress.

So, God, I ask You, not for another promise or prophecy. Your Word is laced with those, and I am grateful for each of them. At this juncture, I need courage and revelation regarding who I am in You and the methods by which to boldly answer destiny's call.

Help me to emerge from this proverbial winepress on purpose and with purpose. There is work to be done — nations to be restored. People to be redeemed. Dead to be resurrected. I cannot be late for the assignment. Clear the path, give me spiritual insight as I surrender to go in Your strength alone.

In Jesus' name,

Amen.

Romans 12:1-2a The Message (MSG)
[1-2a] So here's what I want you to do, God helping you: Take your everyday, ordinary life—your sleeping, eating, going-to-work, and walking-around life—and place it before God as an offering. Embracing what God does for you is the best thing you can do for him.

Who are you seems to be a simple question. As children, we are taught to articulate general facts about ourselves. Parents wildly celebrate when toddlers begin to remember and repeat their names. Even if the words are garbled and almost unintelligible, those mutterings mark a positive step toward knowing and defining oneself.

This trend toward identification perpetuates itself into adolescence. There is, however, a shift from individual identification to peer group identification. Peer groups are the barometer by which most adolescents gauge who they are. They strive to dress alike, use the same vernacular, and listen to the same music. The pursuit during this stage of life is to be like others, to blend in instead of blending out. Establishing a uniqueness is counter middle and school high culture. Thus, during these formative years, many major in identifying *with* instead of being identified individually based on personal character traits and idiosyncrasies.

This paradigm creates a challenge during the shift into adulthood. All of a sudden, the question presented as a toddler – *what is your name?* – returns to the forefront of our interactions. Only this time, what used to be a rite of passage moment is loaded with the potential for a positive or negative judgment. The name exchange represents the gateway to a deeper assessment of the individual. Thus, the essence of the question is not about one's given name, but it is a measuring stick of one's relevance, purpose, and value to others.

Upon entering any new situation, the banter regarding one's point of origin, relatives, friends, and present employment is natural and expected. While one may not be as direct as to ask

"Who are you?" questions such as "What is your name?" or "Where were you born?" represent the usual conversation during an initial encounter. In fact, the absence of such might cause insecurity to develop in a given area. This is indeed the accepted trajectory of most first encounters.

This expectation is not rooted in an invasion of privacy, but it highlights the desire for camaraderie inherent to the human race. At the very least, we have a desire to know something about those with whom we spend time. This knowing makes us more comfortable and provides opportunities for a deeper connection. There is an inclination toward companionship and fellowship that is God-ordained and therefore intrinsic.

Genesis 2:18-24 New International Version (NIV)

The LORD God said, "It is not good for the man to be alone. I will make a helper suitable for him. Now the Lord God had formed out of the ground all the wild animals and all the birds in the sky. He brought them to the man to see what he would name them; and whatever the man called each living creature, that was its name. So the man gave names to all the livestock, the birds in the sky and all the wild animals. But for Adam no suitable helper was found. So the LORD God caused the man to fall into a deep sleep; and while he was sleeping, he took one of the man's ribs and then closed up the place with flesh. Then the LORD God made a woman from the rib he had taken out of the man, and he brought her to the man. The man said, 'This is now bone of my bones and flesh of my flesh; she shall be called 'woman', for she was taken out of man." That is why a man leaves his father and mother and is united to his wife, and they become one flesh.

While this passage of scripture is most often used to highlight God's institution of marriage, it also speaks to the void that materializes when there is no one with whom we can be known and know. We see the best reflection of ourselves as we identify with others. Indeed, Adam was unable to fully know himself until he stood face to face with that which had been in him. His witness of Eve brought him to greater clarity regarding himself, as we see in verses 23-24.

Life-Sustaining Principle

Adam was unable to fully know himself until he stood face to face with that which had been in him.

The same is true for us, as it relates to those around us that usually identify and reflect the essence of our potential. Without your children, you would not see what great parents you are. Without your supervisor, you would not be Employee of the Month. Without your spouse, you would not be a great husband or wife. It is through relationships that potential is identified and nurtured. One way that God reveals our identity to us is through our relationship with others.

Life-Sustaining Principle

It is through relationships that potential is identified and nurtured.

What is interesting, however, is that there is often more attention given to knowing others than knowing ourselves. In fact, gossip is perpetuated because of the ease with which we discuss the business of others. The advice and insight into the lives of others seem to flow easily while the same insight is not evident for ourselves. We know our names, our addresses, and our families. However, when faced with the deeper task of defining ourselves, our purpose, and the path, thereto we may find that we struggle with the question: *Who am I?*

It is so easy to slip into a place of defining oneself based on service to others such as our occupation, our roles as parents, husbands, wives, siblings, etc. Indeed, all of these roles add value to our lives, but they cannot properly define the essence of who we are. If we are to fully address this question, we must start with the definition as found in God's Word.

Genesis 1:27 New International Version (NIV)
So God created mankind in his own image, in the image of God he created them; male and female he created them.

Ephesians 2:10 New International Version (NIV)
For we are God's handiwork, created in Christ Jesus to do good works, which God prepared in advance for us to do.

If we are to embrace the truth of these scriptures, we must reject the contradiction of low self-esteem and feelings of inadequacy. These opposite perspectives cannot operate effectively within the same space. One will eventually override the other. The outcome is based fully on the perspective to which one offers the most attention. Scripture makes it clear that the excellence of the image of God is embedded, if not always expressed, in mankind. God's handiwork is without flaw and far beyond what value the finite mind may endeavor to place on it. As a part of His divine design, God formed Adam from mere dust, an indication of His power to create the most intricate living being in all creation from a substance taken for granted and haphazardly discarded. In essence, God took a thing of no value and made it valuable by virtue of His breath. Therefore, Adam stood before his creator as a perfect reflection of what was in His mind. In His foreknowledge, God ordered it to be so not only for Adam, but for all who would follow. It is this truth that confronts Gideon and forces him to make a choice – his perception, or God's. While thoughts of fear and failure ricochet through Gideon's mind, he must make an active decision, followed by definite action, to reject every thought opposite of what he heard from the angel messenger. If he was to respond in the affirmative to the call and assignment on his life God's perception was the only one that he could allow to dominate. To give credence to anything less would most assuredly subvert the victory.

Introducing the Man of the Hour

Judges 6:11 introduces the reader to Gideon. His name has not been mentioned in scripture prior, but his persona erupts into Biblical history under a powerful mandate and declaration. The angel alerts Gideon to two facts: the Lord is with him, and he is a mighty warrior (man of valor). Both of these declarations belie the reality of Gideon's life. First of all, everything about Israel's situation indicates that God is *not* with them. He was, however, definitely with them. It was the presence and power of God that had sustained Israel to that point. Their view of God's presence was skewed because of their disobedience and His response to it. So often, when the believer is chastised by God, they assume the victim role, as if God has deserted them. Such a posture hinders correcting the wrong and has the potential to further separate one from the God of their salvation. The Bible is clear that God's discipline comes to those He loves, and His love is a definite manifestation of His presence.

There have been many times that I have felt an absence of God's presence. Upon honest examination of my life, I found that God had not moved, but instead, I drifted. In college, I experienced this feeling of an absence of God. However, when I stopped and examined my lifestyle, I was forced to admit that my disobedience had driven me from God and that the consequences thereof were purposed to drive me back to Him. The tight spot was ordained to drive me back to the right spot.

And so it was with Gideon and his countrymen. Israel found themselves in extreme turmoil and poverty because of their refusal to obey God. It seems that they struggled continuously with consistency. They would be faithful to God for a period of time only to be swayed into idolatry by their surroundings. Paul explained it thus, "Be not deceived: evil communication corrupts good manner" (I Corinthians 15:33 KJV). One must be mindful of the company that you keep. Attributed to Benjamin Franklin's Poor Richard's Almanac and quoted by grandmothers all over the world the old adage, "If you lay down with dogs you will get up with fleas" offers a picture of Israel's perpetual cycle of sin, judgment, and repentance. Evil company had Israel in a horrible place.

What Gideon did not know was that he was the man of the hour. He was the man that God had ordained to deliver His people from the oppression of that season. Gideon's inability to see himself through God's lens forced him into a perpetual state of fear and could have caused him to miss his destiny assignment.

What is a Destiny Assignment?

Like Gideon, we all have a destiny assignment – a reason for which we have been born, something that only we can do and people whose lives hang in the balance until we cease fighting and make a decision to fulfill destiny. The predestined or predetermined plan of God for one's life is never to be taken lightly, as the God of love purposes to reflect Himself through us. This reflection is illuminated for the world by the work that we do and the passion with which we approach our God-given assignments.

As was the case with Gideon, fear is often the default reaction to the enormity of God's assignment on a life. However, as it becomes clear that God's handiwork is a perfect work, accepting that He wills His best through yielded vessels becomes the source for the necessary empowerment to respond properly to the call of destiny. This aspect of the journey is a transformation, a metamorphosis of sorts, but the outcome is many souls saved alive.

When Fear Causes Compromise

However, first, fear must be confronted and progressively conquered. The power of God and fear cannot flow in the same space. Fear brings torment, and God's spirit releases liberty. This absence of harassment and release of freedom usher in anointing for confidence and provokes spirit-led action.

1 John 4:18 King James Version (KJV)
There is no fear in love; but perfect love casteth out fear: because fear hath torment. He that feareth is not made perfect in love.

2 Corinthians 3:17 King James Version (KJV)
Now the Lord is that Spirit: and where the Spirit of the Lord is, there is liberty.

In order to arrive in this place, Gideon's habits of thinking and being must change. Notice, even the method in which Gideon carried out his daily activity was motivated by fear. He was threshing wheat in the winepress. The winepress was the place where grapes were gathered and crushed, usually by foot, for the production of wine. Like the threshing floor, it was a place of production and a place that necessitated the exertion of a considerable amount of physical strength.

Life-Sustaining Principle

The power of God and fear cannot flow in the same space. Fear brings torment, and God's spirit releases liberty.

Yet, the fact remains that the winepress was not the designated place for the threshing of wheat. It was a good substitute, but it did not represent the best venue in which to carry out the activity of separating the wheat from the chaff.

Threshing was hard and tedious work, and it involved continual swinging of the arms. The nature of this work indicates that Gideon was not a lazy man. In fact, his name means destroyer or hewer. By virtue of his name, he possessed the physical prowess for war and victory. His name made him a leader; all he had to do was live up to the declaration that was made each time his name was called. When someone said, "Good morning Gideon," what the atmosphere heard was, "Good morning *Destroyer*."

So often, fear will motivate us to ungodly compromise. Fear will cause us to do the *right thing* with the *wrong people* and expect the *right results*. But at the root of that fear is a failure to recognize who we are in Christ and the power that we share with Him through the new birth. In steps the grace of God to remind us that our ways and His ways are eons apart. (Isaiah 55:9)

Ephesians 2:8 King James Version (KJV)
For by grace are ye saved through faith; and that not of yourselves: it is the gift of God:

Isaiah 55:9 King James Version (KJV)
For as the heavens are higher than the earth, so are my ways higher than your ways, and my thoughts than your thoughts.

Gideon was by no means weak or fragile; he was just scared, and because of fear, he found himself doing the *right thing* in the *wrong place*. Despite the fact that Gideon had allowed fear to cause him to do the right thing in the wrong place, the grace of God searched for him and found him in that wrong place. He saw Gideon, sent a heavenly ambassador to Gideon, and released Gideon into his divine assignment.

Likewise, the grace of God finds us in our wrong places. He calls our names and certifies His choice of us by virtue of the anointing He releases on our lives for our Kingdom assignment.

Neither our fears nor failures hinder the ultimate will of God for our lives.

Life-Sustaining Principle

The grace of God finds us in our wrong places. He calls our names and certifies His choice of us by virtue of the anointing He releases on our lives for our Kingdom assignment.

Divine Visitation Resulting in Divine Revelation

With the divine visitation came divine revelation. While it did not come in an instant, Gideon began to view himself in a different light. He was still standing in the winepress, but his mindset was being challenged. He was being transformed by the renewing of his mind, and what he thought began to manifest as his thoughts motivated his actions.

Romans 12:2 King James Version (KJV)
And be not conformed to this world: but be ye transformed by the renewing of your mind, that ye may prove what is that good, and acceptable, and perfect, will of God.

Revelation, identity, and purpose were downloaded into Gideon, and he was moved from a place of fear and into a place of extreme faith. At that moment, Gideon's excuses became inexcusable. His background was irrelevant. God had a purpose for his life beyond anything that he could have thought about himself.

Every morning you keep asking yourself the question, "Who am I and why am I here?." The answer is in the mouth of the Lord. When God speaks, He speaks to purpose, and there is nothing like a Word of purpose spoken over your life. With purpose comes assignment.

Like Gideon, there is something for you to do, and for you to change. There is a condition for you to rectify. The challenge of poverty, immorality, and violence are going to be solved by people who accept the challenge as Gideon did. This generation groans for the courageous Gideons to mentor, tutor, and train them, but you have to leave the winepress and embrace your encounter with the Lord. Who you are is in His mouth! Your ear must be found pressed to His mouth in order to clearly hear what He desires for and of you.

The definition of who you are must originate with God and be found through His Word. He will search for you in all of your wrong places. He will meet you where you are even when you have good intentions but are operating from a wrong place. He found the Apostle Paul on the road to Damascus in a similar state. He wholeheartedly believed that he was serving a God purpose. The truth of the matter, however, was that he was employing the wrong methods and with the wrong people. That encounter ushered Paul into a place of God revelation and started him on a journey of knowing himself and the reason for which he was created.

Understand, the spiritual search party God sends out for you is for one purpose – to reveal your Kingdom assets and your Kingdom assignment. God is going to place you in your divine assignment because it is there that your proper identity will be made clear.

You have defaulted to others looking for them to define you to you. You have looked to your parents to define you. You have looked to relationships to define you. You have looked to organizations to define you. You have looked to your religious community to define you. You have gained titles and degrees and still struggle to articulate and manifest the essence of who God ordained for you to be. Know this. It is only through a God encounter that clarity regarding destiny emerges. Gideon walked away from that encounter with an identity shift. The Lord gave him an assignment and the resources with which to complete it.

Gideon was not an overnight success. In fact, he stumbled and struggled at points until his death. Our society is pervasive with overnight wonders, but they are most often here today and gone tomorrow. Destiny takes time; it has to be cultivated under the watchful eye of mentors, pastors, and leaders and then birthed out by personal visitation of the Holy Ghost. Gideon went through this process numerous times as his purpose and assignment evolved. Because he submitted himself to the process, we never see Gideon hiding in the winepress again. He experiences an authentic identity shift. Such an experience catapults one into destiny. He leaves the wrong place and takes courage to do his assigned right thing in view of the public.

Life-Sustaining Principle

Destiny takes time; it has to be cultivated under the watchful eye of mentors, pastors, and leaders and then birthed out by personal visitation of the Holy Ghost.

Gideon learned to do it afraid. He learned that God created him to be a world changer. He learned that his family, his nation, and preordained destiny were waiting on him to lead a rebellion and effect lasting change. Gideon learned that the people he was sent to help would not always support him. Some of them would even desert him. He learned that the assignment was his, and there would be times of loneliness and frustration. But none of those things had the power to alter his destiny or remove the anointing to carry it out.

Life-Sustaining Principle

Experiencing an authentic identity shift catapults one into destiny.

Gideon accepted that he was indeed a mighty man of valor. He saw through a revelatory vision that God was yet with Israel, and that He had not neglected His covenant with His special people. Though Gideon was considered the least in his natural father's eyes, God had an extreme plan for him. Once Gideon heard and heeded the voice of the Lord identifying who he was, he was irrevocably changed.

Questions:

1. How does your image of yourself challenge or support God's definition of who you are?

   _____

   _____

   _____

   _____

   _____

2. What Gideon type task has God called you to?

   _____

   _____

   _____

3. How are you preparing yourself mentally and emotionally to properly fulfill destiny?

   _____

   _____

   _____

   _____

4. Where is your proverbial winepress? Where are you hiding?

_____

_____

_____

_____

_____

5. If you answered yes, to the second question in number 4, what will coming out of hiding "cost" you?

_____

_____

_____

_____

_____

6. Take a moment and identify 3-5 Destiny Assignments that you have already embarked upon.

_____

_____

_____

_____

_____

7. Take a moment and identify 3-5 Destiny Assignments that you plan to embark upon, but have yet to start.

_____

_____

_____

_____

_____

8. Identify people in your life that may be able to serve as mentors as you move further in your Kingdom assignment. Use the answers from number 7 to identify individuals who may be of assistance.

_____

_____

_____

_____

_____

_____

Chapter 5
Moving Beyond, "IF God be for us."
by Ebony Green

Scripture: Judges 6:12-16 KJV

[12] And the angel of the LORD appeared unto him, and said unto him, The LORD is with thee, thou mighty man of valour. [13] And Gideon said unto him, Oh my Lord, if the LORD be with us, why then is all this befallen us? and where be all his miracles which our fathers told us of, saying, Did not the LORD bring us up from Egypt? but now the LORD hath forsaken us, and delivered us into the hands of the Midianites. [14] And the LORD looked upon him, and said, Go in this thy might, and thou shalt save Israel from the hand of the Midianites: have not I sent thee? [15] And he said unto him, Oh my Lord, wherewith shall I save Israel? behold, my family is poor in Manasseh, and I am the least in my father's house. [16] And the LORD said unto him, Surely I will be with thee, and thou shalt smite the Midianites as one man.

Prayer

*Father, thank You for the reminder that You are ahead, constantly walking with us, and the blood of Jesus covers our behind. Today, we stand in the spiritually mature and developed place of not "**IF**" God be for us, but "**When**" God is for us – we always win! We praise You for defeat over specious mentalities that have caused trepidation, lack, and superfluous torment. Our now and eternal declaration is…because God is for us, He is more than the entire world against us. Your "word" has settled everything in our "worlds" and made it so. Thank You for rest and moving us beyond the "ifs" of our life's giants.*

In Jesus Name,

Amen.

Learning to Remain Steadfast in God's Word

Certain characteristics were apparent in Gideon as he was faced with the "giants" of his day. Gideon, like many believers, sought answers from God in regard to his approach to a seemingly impossible situation. God responded to Gideon's inquiries with *affirmation*, a word of *victory,* and *strategy*.

God's *affirmation* to Gideon was, *"The Lord is with you, you mighty man of valor!"* God called Gideon a man of "valor," which means fearless or bold. Bold may have been the opposite of Gideon's sentiment, but God was letting him know he could take courage and operate this way because God was with him. Failure is not an option when God is ahead of you; His presence marks your future with an automatic win.

Secondly, God gave Gideon _strategy_. *Then the Lord turned to him and said, "**Go** in this thy might…"* The strategy that God gave Gideon was to **GO**. He was instructing Gideon with one word to allow him to move beyond all of the previous "IF" statements –and to know with assurance that God had already marked his future with victory. God's "GO" strategy is as simple as the command. We must move on His word. The details are often completed in the process of your obedient move. However, you can move forward in peace knowing that at the end of GO is "success" marked by God because He sanctioned the move.

God's "go" divine strategy:

Allow me to share a personal experience. In a specific vision, a woman of God spoke to me regarding attending school again and establishing schools. I had several subsequent open visions which included teaching children, formulating schools and politics. God even gave me a name in one dream of someone who would help me in this educational process. Initially, I thought this cannot be right I need to go back to sleep. I was seven years post grade school education and law school which was more than enough to me, why do I need to teach? I thought I was supposed to be a lawyer? However, I trusted the voice of God. *God quickly showed me that although I trusted His voice, I didn't trust His strategy.* Subsequently, a Prophet came in alignment with the very words God had revealed to me by sharing he saw me in business and working with children and schools all around. A Bishop shared in the prior year, she saw me not only teaching but also practicing in New York. My analytical brain kicked into overdrive and tried to make it happen, ultimately formulating my strategy to the plan that God voiced. I researched New York graduate schools for education and began to draft plans for this business. However, I found nothing. I was confused because I thought it was "go" time.

What I learned, with God's GO strategy, there is nothing you have to "do" per se except believe. Subsequently, God will give you the exact steps when it is time. Thanksgiving 2015, God sent me a vision of eagles flying north and some fellow parishioners planning my going away gift. He shared in the vision that I would be moving, and He gave me the exact date January 25, 2016. Those were the only words I received, and it was less than two months away! I had received a promotion at my current job and another department wanted to hire me with a significant pay increase, this position would have been perfect for my legal career. Nonetheless, I knew this was not God's plan. Again, I erroneously tried to make it happen and teach since that's what God said the plan was. I went on an interview to be a professor and they hired me. Within 24 hours, they called back to say the job would actually begin March 2016.

Then I became even more frustrated because I knew I was not in alignment with His will and I was ready to go! I then heard, "follow MY plan." I knew God told me that I was to go to school on 1/25/16 in New York and it would be very cold. December 6, 2015, I googled what graduate schools begin January 25 in New York? Only one non-online graduate school came up, Buffalo State. I knew for certain this was His GO time.

Less than two weeks later, I was accepted into Buffalo State. Without a "guaranteed" job, any family or friends in the city, I planned my move and attempted to leave the 22nd of January. However, a bad snowstorm occurred; so, just as God said it would happen, I took a flight on January 25, 2016. As the plane ascended and I saw the birds flying, I remembered God's words and vision to me on Thanksgiving 2015. By that evening, I was in my first graduate level education course.

The name God gave me in the prior dream, ended up being my first boss, when I saw his name on the door, I knew to apply. He ultimately helped me finish my in-class teaching certification. God had it all planned. I was working within one month, in my own house within four months, the "global ministries" that was prophesied to me before my departure by Pastor Yasha Becton was the church that covered me during my duration, He had people aligned that were like family during my time there and He even connected me with a beautician with roots to South Carolina (yes, a stylist is important). Less than three years later, I obtained the third degree (Masters of Education in Early Childhood and Childhood), I am working full time in the business He gave me in the state where He gave me to begin, I am on one of the U.S. Commission boards for South Carolina and I use all my education under my company.

There were many doubters regarding whether this was God's "go" especially when God told me to return home to start a business in South Carolina and there were countless conquests I had to endure during the process. To be honest, one of the doubters was me, not about moving to another state, just the plan when I was there. I knew teaching came natural and the idea was not foreign. On the contrary, I could not see myself "traditionally" teaching in a classroom. How did this align with a legal career or business, which seem more fitting to my identity? I later discovered the answers to those questions but like Chapter four reminds us of Gideon doing it scared, so did I. I trusted God's "go" and that the "sense" of it all was in the mix and I would discover it one day.

Success is always manifested at the "end" of God's go. The "go" strategy is different for all of us. With me, it is a slow work. Since childhood, my earthly father would remind me "patience is a virtue" because I wanted things upon request. When others hear God say go, it may be immediate to build confidence or whatever the reason. God knows the needs of His children, do not compare your go to anyone else's go from God, it will not be the same as we all have different ids. We have to trust His divine strategy even if it is not how others or even ourselves originally id'd us. There is nothing you have to "do," only believe and He will guide your footsteps along the way and make sense of His id.

Lastly, God gave Gideon _victory_, "..._you shall save Israel from the hand of the Midianites. Have I not sent you?"_ (Judges 6:14b KJV). God told Gideon that he was going to defeat his enemy and more importantly, that God was sending him. This last inquiry served as a reminder that God being in your "ahead" is more than the entire world against you (Romans 8:31).

Gideon, like many of us, wanted more signs (and more words) than the concise few words from God of *affirmation*, *strategy*, and *victory*. One obvious trait Gideon possessed initially was "wavering" faith. One of the fortunate attributes of living in this era is that we have so many examples of God doing exactly what He said. In other words, God has a track record of never failing. Thousands of generations have passed, and many believers still struggle with resting and subsequently growing beyond, "**IF** God be for us." God, in countless moments, shared in the Bible where He was already ahead –in our future places, i.e., the book of Revelation. Therefore, when God speaks, it already is. His words are not a "deliberation," they are a final resting place. So, whether God speaks one word or thousands of words, whatever He said shall be.

Life-Sustaining Principle

Therefore, when God speaks, it already is. His words are not a "deliberation," they are a final resting place.

When is "Enough" final?

God told Gideon that He was with him. Yet, Gideon attempted to move ahead of God by telling God his current predicament, *"O my Lord, if the Lord is with us, why then has all this happened to us? And where are all His miracles, which our fathers told us about, saying, 'Did not the Lord bring us up from Egypt?"* Gideon further voiced the seeming impossibility of the situation. *"O my Lord, how can I save Israel? Indeed my clan is the weakest in Manasseh, and I am the least in my father's house."*

Believers, we have to learn to remain steadfast in God's word.

Isaiah 55:8-9 (KJV)
For my thoughts are not your thoughts, neither are your ways my ways, saith the Lord. For as the heavens are higher than the

earth, so are my ways higher than your ways, and my thoughts than your thoughts.

Do not allow words that have not manifested YET or the vision of your NOW to thwart your belief in God. This, simply put, is a place of <u>maturity</u>. We know there are different sizes of faith by the "mustard" seed faith description in Matthew 17:20. I have found giving God's Word time, continuing to follow Christ, and remaining steadfast will inevitably cause your faith to grow. This path will cause you to move from a seed to a root, and then a plant, until you are fully blossoming in every season.

Life-Sustaining Principle

I have found giving God's Word time, continuing to follow Christ, and remaining steadfast will inevitably cause your faith to grow.

Moving Beyond IF

God is FAITHFUL to what He says. God's words are promises. When He speaks, it is **settled** in heaven. Therefore, the language of "IF" is erroneous (Mark 9:23). It is already known that God is for us because He said He is. Learn from Gideon in these verses. Know God is always for you. It is not a pondering of "if," but always acknowledge that God's words shall perform in His way (Isaiah 55:8-9) and time (Habakkuk 2:2-3). Move beyond, **IF** God be for us.

Life-Sustaining Principle

The language of "IF" is erroneous (Mark 9:23). It is already known that God is for us because He said He is…Know God is always for you.

Change your language to "**when**" He performs… always have an air of expectancy concerning the word of the Lord. Moving beyond the "if" requires becoming rooted in God's words while simultaneously sending a command for His words to "*author*" your now.

Envision the process of a plant. First, there is a seed (the word from God), as you water the seed a root begins to sprout above ground (Faith), as the plant is continuously nurtured (fed the word of God), the plant begins to grow. One word from God sends a command for production and growth "beyond" where the word commenced. As we explore this topic, there are 4 points that I would like to share.

Point 1: Who does God say you are?

Judges 6:12 (KJV)
And the angel of the LORD appeared unto him, and said unto him, The LORD is with thee, thou mighty man of valor.

Gideon was facing an army that exceeded his men in number and strength. As a result, Gideon inaccurately decided that a lethal ending was the likely outcome for him. At this point, Gideon accepted the allusion that comparison brings. God sees us for His designed and *expected* ending (Jeremiah 29:11). Therefore, instead of analyzing what's not, we have to adopt what is.

Gideon's destiny was written. God called him a man of valor. Valor denotes fearlessness, boldness, courage, or heroism. The best way to defeat an "allusion" of an ostensibly erroneous fate is to re-write the narrative with the word of God. Gideon went through unnecessary self-torment because God already said he would be victorious.

Life-Changing Principle

The best way to defeat an "allusion" of an ostensibly erroneous fate is to re-write the narrative with the word of God.

In life, we will all have, or are currently facing, some "giants." Giants can be real-life enemies, finances, insecurities, relationship issues, or general life/spiritual struggles that threaten the quintessence of who God has said we are. **IF** these giants persist without our extermination of them, they can torment the essence of who we know we are and cause us to accept a narrative that God did not write for our lives.

Please understand, there is a "persistent attack" on who God says you are. There is often a battle between our flesh and the enemy. The enemy states the opposite of truth or whatever God has declared. In moments of intimidation or trying times, if we are not careful, we may accept the language of Satan. This perception can become so real that it distorts what God has clearly spoken to us.

These thoughts must first be recognized and subsequently thrown out of our minds (2 Corinthians 10:3-5).

Identity shifts are evident but often accepted in children who daily vary between being a fairy or superman. However, the vacillation in identity can become a problem when the child begins to emulate beliefs or standards that contradict the *word* of the Lord, or who He has called him or her to be. The parent or guardian has to draw a line in the sand between a child simply developing, i.e., "child's play" or when there is an attack on the child's identity – who God has called the child to be. Some adult believers are still holding fast to "child's play."

1 Corinthians 13:11
*When I was a child, I spake as a child, I understood as a child, I thought as a child: but when I became a man, I **put** away childish things.*

Gideon was not only facing an army; he was the leader. Some circumstances call for us to **put** down "childish" ways, sayings, or beliefs. "I am a babe in Christ; so, I can falter often." "This situation is too big for me." We must all step fully into our God-given identities. Gideon needed to put away child-like practices by recognizing God has a track record of always winning. He designs perfect endings from the beginning.

Therefore, all mentalities or thoughts contrary to God's affirmation that Gideon is a man of valor and victorious was recognized as child's play. He needed to move beyond the early development stage of small seed faith and accept only in his mind who God said he was.

Who Does God Say YOU Are?

First, "*And the angel of the Lord appeared unto him,*" Judges 6:12. Stop reading and meditate on this sentence. How many of you reading have had an angelic visitation when dealing with your named "giant?" If you are one of the fortunate few of this minority, has the visitation occurred every single time you tackled a matter of great magnitude? More than likely, not for the average person.

Therefore, if nothing else brings you solace about what is to come in your turmoil, an angel of the Lord appearing before you should do this.

If you still need help, please know that:

God's word is final.

"...The Lord is with thee, thou mighty man of valor."

The angel of the Lord gave Gideon the assurance that God was with him. Then the Lord identified who Gideon was, "*a mighty man of valor.*" You can find rest in your God-given identity. There are no alterations. Your God-identity is FINAL. You may grow further into it, but the id will never change. It is who you are. Gideon could rest in God's given identity because despite what he felt or saw, God's strength was upon him.

Life-Sustaining Principle

Your God-identity is FINAL. You may grow further into it, but the id will never change. It is who you are.

---

2 Corinthians 12:8-10
*For this thing I besought the Lord thrice that it might depart from me. And he said unto me, My grace is sufficient for thee: for my strength is made perfect in weakness. Most gladly, therefore, will I rather glory in my infirmities, that **the power of Christ may rest upon me**. Therefore I take pleasure in infirmities, in reproaches, in necessities, in persecutions, in distresses for Christ's sake: for when I am weak, then am I strong.*

God said He was "mighty," meaning Gideon had "power." Not just any power, but the power of Christ rested upon him as soon as the words were released from the Lord. Therefore, Gideon should have boasted, "yes, their army may be larger or even stronger, but God has called me mighty. It is settled in heaven. I am triumphant."

You may not get an angelic visitation, but God has not only spoken about your circumstance, He has given you HIS identity.

Who has God declared you to be?

The above sentence is not a rhetorical question. Ask God.

Prayer

Father, You know my giant of the day. But I know You are with me and will never leave (Deuteronomy 31:6). Who do You say I am, Father? Teach me today and forever, Father. So, I never falter in faith or my God-given identity. What is Your quest for me today?

Point 2: Do not let circumstances cloud your placement

Judges 6:13

And Gideon said unto him, oh my Lord, if the Lord be with us, why then is all this befallen us? And where be all his miracles, which our fathers told us of, saying, did not the Lord bring us from Egypt? But now the Lord hath forsaken us and delivered us into the hands of the Midianites.

Here, Gideon allowed his "circumstances" to cloud his placement. Do you remember whom Gideon was talking to? An angel of the Lord! God had given Gideon a heavenly placement.

Ephesians 2:6

And hath raised us up together, and made us sit together in heavenly places in Christ Jesus:

As believers, we must understand, when we go up, we never *have to* come down! God has seated you in heavenly places

86

with Christ. In this place, you can truly depend on Him without wavering. Place an indelible "period" when you know the Father has instructed—and wait on God. Meditate on His word. Move only when you are certain God has sanctioned the utterance. And no matter what –wait on God.

Although, you are dealing with Giants, i.e., life vicissitudes, do not forget God has you seated in heavenly places. Do not come down out of your seat to "assess" the land. This will only "cloud" your perception. You are seated in Heavenly places. Come high, remain there, and do not search low.

Point 3: Whose Voice Do You SEE?

Words shape our worlds.
HIS word fulfills promises.

Judges 6:14 (KJV)
And the Lord looked upon him, and said, go in this thy might, and thou shalt save Israel from the hand of the Midianites: have not I sent thee?

Words shape our worlds. Proverbs 18:21 tells us the power of life and death is in the tongue. We often emphasize the *life* or *death* mentioned in this verse. But POWER is the driving force of this verse. Words have power. Your tongue is promoting one thing or the other. LIFE or death. You can only be sure *what* to speak

87

by the power of the Holy Ghost. God's word shaped this world literally since the beginning of time, and we still SEE it today. He spoke light, and there was (Genesis 1:3).

God's words fulfill promises. His word is the promise. Think about your life and recall one thing God spoke and it was. "That is enough..." that is enough to move you beyond **IF** God be for us. He has a track record since the beginning of time, Genesis to Revelation; He has proven in your life and mine to do ALL He says according to Philippians 1:6.

The Lord is speaking directly to Gideon in verse 14. He reminded Gideon of his "might." He reminded Gideon that GOD sent him. What else is there to question? Finally, the Lord gave the outcome. ISRAEL WILL BE DEFEATED. In other words, it was settled in heaven.

God "grew" Gideon in this dialogue. He could move beyond IF God was for him because he knew now. He was talking to him, giving him a strategy and the end result. God does the same with us. He tells us the end from the beginning.

Habakkuk 2:3

For the vision is yet for an appointed time, but at the end it shall speak, and not lie: though it tarry, wait for it; because it will surely come, it will not tarry.

Then in time and/or when we ask, God gives *strategy* to accomplish what is already settled with Him. Are you still wavering on what God has settled for you? You may need to switch voices. Allow God's voice to be the only voice and "shaper" of your world. You should be able to look at your "giant" or circumstance and SEE what God sees because He shapes your world.

SEEING and HEARING moves you beyond "**IF**" God be with us. "**If**" changes and our language becomes "**when**..." God does what He says; thusly, "expanding" or "growing" your language to a place of authority where your world manifests God's word. You have to learn to operate in the authority you have been given. What is your authority? To speak and declare what His heart is commanding, desiring, or saying. There should be evidence of what you have spoken Manifesting in the now — declaring the POWER of God. If you are coming in the name of the Lord, timidity is out. POWER and Holy boldness are in. Make declarations and believe. Evidence will occur.

God's word is more powerful than your work assessment.

Your hardest working moment cannot equate to a one-word release from God. Living in the dispensation of Grace is a reminder that there is nothing we can "do" to qualify, promote, or keep us at a certain place. Jesus "did" it all. Therefore, exuding all your time, energy, and/or resources into matters will not always cause advancement. However, when God steps in and speaks a word of favor over the same situation you have been working on, everything instantly changes. Of course, God wants us to work diligently on what He has mandated but learn to rest when we identify His voice in our situation. When God speaks, you have to see what He said, before the actual physical manifestation.

When you are in the heart of a matter, and God speaks a word of victory, take rest and *see* that your most diligent moment does not equate to the word God just spoke over you. Do you believe it? Live it NOW! God's word shifts us to a place of automatic authority.

Life-Sustaining Principle

Your hardest working moment cannot equate to one-word release from God.

Authority is the power or right to give orders, make decisions, and enforce obedience. You have the power to change circumstances in the lives of others and yours. POWER is granted. You have the authority to make decisions and place commands on your circumstances. People with true authority have a "presence," their name and "might" precedes them. They do not compete with voices. There is no power struggle. You obey the command or leave.

Gideon was leading with fear by comparing his status, seeing the seemingly large number of the enemy's camp, and forgetting all God had "already" spoken. Gideon "saw" the voice of fear, which does not derive from God. In these verses, he allowed trepidation to shape his world, and he was not walking in his God-given authority.

Fearful leaders or those who lead with fear seldom remain in power.

Gideon needed to use his authority at that moment to "enforce" the ineffaceable truths God had sanctioned. He could

90

have overcome fear by pronouncing God's word of victory, which would have altered in his perception; thusly, shaping his world to line up with God's prophetic release.

Eradicate all fear. Know whose voice shapes your world and monopolize in true authority. Doing all of these things will allow you to always "see" God's voice in your circumstances. Speaking God's word is an "active" practice that "activates" His life-giving words to a place of authority that molds your matters in alignment with God's truth.

Point 4: Beyond the veil...eliminating the enemy of doubt from our language.

Judges 6:15 (KJV)
And he said unto him, oh my Lord, where with shall I have Israel? Behold my family is poor in Manasseh and I am least in my father's house.

With all the affirmation, Gideon still did not believe. He doubted the words of God. Gideon had an angelic visitation, God spoke to him, God not only told him you are going to win, but He gave him the strategy to accomplish it all.

Our society promotes an inquisitive nature. There is a theory that asking plentiful questions promotes knowledge. In reality, when you ask God numerous questions that HE has already responded to in the Bible or in a word directly to you, it only reveals you are struggling with the enemy doubt. You will either prolong your time in fighting this battle and/or frustrate the process with your speculations or "ways" on trying to help God out.

Gideon did not have to tell God his family was poor or that he was the least in his father's house. If Gideon studied the Father, he would have found rest in his lowly place as God has a pattern to be auspicious to those who are thought of as least, the unexpected, or non-traditional. People will have to acknowledge in their success that it was God who did that! Doubt is eliminated with these types of circumstances. Gideon overlooked his identity. The Lord called him *mighty*.

Gideon disregarded his *placement*, he was seated in heavenly places with Christ, and the socioeconomic status of his family was futile information.

Have you ever been a Gideon in a major circumstance?

Have you ever been faced with something that seemed unmanageable like having more bills than money, a generational health issue that plagued you, or God saying you will be triumphant at something that you have failed many times attempting to succeed?

You receive words of encouragement, prophecies, and direction from the Lord. But to you, you still saw a GIANT. If we all could just move beyond the veil…it WILL eliminate that enemy of doubt. I am going to take you beyond Gideon's veil where the Lord was pushing him.

The Lord already spoke – so it is settled. If Gideon remained in his "heavenly seat," he would have known what was beyond the veil.

Jeremiah 33:3 (KJV)
Call unto me, and I will answer thee, and show thee great and mighty things, which thou knowest not.

God is the Lord of Hosts. This translates to angel armies. When the enemy ups his troops against you, a higher standard is raised against him and legions of ministering angels are sent out to fight on your behalf.

Hebrews 1:14 (KJV)
Are they not all ministering spirits, sent forth to minister for them who shall be heirs of salvation?

Gideon just needed to remain seated, and he would have seen beyond the veil, with all the angels fighting on his behalf. Know that God is with you. Keep your heavenly seat, sup with the Father, and watch the Lord of hosts fight on your behalf!

Questions

1. Identify God's word about your current season. What is the Holy Spirit speaking to you?

   _____

   _____

   _____

   _____

2. What are your giants during this period of time?

   _____

   _____

   _____

   _____

   _____

3. How are you handling these giants from a "spiritually mature" place?

   _____

   _____

   _____

   _____

   _____

4. What are the three ways God alerted Gideon that He was for him (Hint: A.S.V.)?

    _____

    _____

    _____

    _____

5. What God indicators in your life display His presence in your circumstance?

    _____

    _____

    _____

    _____

6. What are some "childish" practices that have hindered your development in believing what God says?

    _____

    _____

    _____

    _____

7. What are the two ways to handle attacks on the word of God for your now (Hint: book title & 2 Corinthians 10:4-5)?

    _____

    _____

    _____

    _____

8. How do you live in a place of authority?

_____

_____

_____

_____

9. How does moving beyond the veil in worship (Exodus 26:31; Hebrews 10:19-22) correlate to moving beyond the veil in your circumstance?

_____

_____

_____

_____

Chapter 6
Employing Your Secret Weapons: Declarations, Offerings, and Altars
by Yasha Jones Becton

Scripture: Judges 6:17-24 KJV

> 17 And he said unto him, If now I have found grace in thy sight, then shew me a sign that thou talkest with me. 18 Depart not hence, I pray thee, until I come unto thee, and bring forth my present, and set it before thee. And he said, I will tarry until thou come again. 19 And Gideon went in, and made ready a kid, and unleavened cakes of an ephah of flour: the flesh he put in a basket, and he put the broth in a pot, and brought it out unto him under the oak, and presented it. 20 And the angel of God said unto him, Take the flesh and the unleavened cakes, and lay them upon this rock, and pour out the broth. And he did so. 21 Then the angel of the LORD put forth the end of the staff that was in his hand, and touched the flesh and the unleavened cakes; and there rose up fire out of the rock, and consumed the flesh and the unleavened cakes. Then the angel of the LORD departed out of his sight.

Prayer

Father, as I mature in my walk with You, help me to pursue a walk that is pleasing in your sight. You have been so gracious towards me. Yet, I have wasted so much time in aimless pursuits. I can never repay You for all that You have done for me. But I CAN offer You my life as a living sacrifice unto you. I CAN pursue Your divine will with fervor, urgency, and expectation. I CAN identify unique and meaningful ways to express my love towards you. As I live out the remainder of my days, my heart longs to please you. My heart's desire is to establish You as my forever number one. Teach me to number my days so that I might gain a heart of wisdom. Father, help me to give no further attention to what I didn't do or where I missed the mark, but help me to focus on what I CAN DO NOW to express my love to You.

In Jesus Name, I pray.

Amen.

Recently, I asked my husband, "How can I love you better?" I was a bit taken aback when he had a well-prepared (almost rehearsed) answer. He shared with me a few suggestions, along with a short list of dos and don'ts. I was shocked, embarrassed, and almost stunned. While it is a bit funny to me now, I was obviously bitten by the "pride" bug.

Oftentimes, in love relationships, we naturally assume that we are doing a great job at loving the other person. This is one of the reasons being married is such a challenge. It takes a certain level of maturity to examine our expressions of love towards another person. I often share that we cannot help but to see others. Yet, looking in the mirror at ourselves requires a deliberate decision. Further, it takes an even deeper level of maturity to listen to constructive feedback in an effort to determine how to take any given love relationship to an even deeper level of commitment.

That's what I want to explore in this chapter; How to move your relationship with God to an even deeper level of commitment. When we first give our lives to Christ, we rejoice in seeing our prayers answered immediately!!! He lets us know that He is truly an ever-present help. It's not until we move into discipleship that we begin to understand that we too have a role to play and responsibilities to fulfill in our relationship with God. Then, once we begin to walk in our calling, we learn that there is yet more that will be required of us.

Intimacy with God will foster clarity, definition, and revelation about your true identity. The closer we are to God, the more He is able to reveal to us who we really are. The angel reveals to Gideon in an intimate moment that he is a mighty man of valor. Up until this point, he was obviously unaware.

Life-Sustaining Principle

Intimacy with God will foster clarity, definition, and revelation about your true identity.

Oftentimes, as believers, we overlook or refuse to carefully examine the level of love expression we offer God. While we can never be as loving to Him as He is towards us, this does not mean that we should not make a lifelong commitment to offering Him the highest expression of our love.

In this chapter, I want to explore three expressions of love that are guaranteed to catapult your spiritual walk and elevate you to a place all Christians should aspire to be. These expressions of love, exercised in faith and sincerity, will continuously cultivate intimacy in your love and devotion to God. The three love expressions include declarations, offerings, and altars. As it is with each of these love expressions, we are not posturing ourselves to determine what we can get from God. Rather, we are taking the more mature posture of determining what we can offer or express to God.

The Psalmist asked the question in Psalm 116:12 (KJV), "What shall I render unto the Lord for all His benefits toward me?" The Psalmist follows his question with the answer. He says, "I will take the cup of salvation, and call upon the name of the Lord. I will pay my vows unto the Lord now in the presence of all his people" (Psalm 116:13-14).

First, He Must Be Received

The Psalmist writes, "I will take the cup of salvation." In other words, he is going to first receive the offer of salvation. Before we examine how we can express our love to Christ, we must first receive Him. By receiving the offer of salvation, we receive the one who is offering salvation to us. We come into agreement with His will and His plan for our lives. This is paramount. It is impossible to elevate a relationship that has yet to be secured or solidified through agreement. This is one of the errors of our day. We try to create a future prior to establishing a covenant. Houses are built after the foundation has been poured and solidified. Sometimes we want to determine the size of the structure prior to ensuring the strength and depth of the foundation.

Life-Sustaining Principle

It is impossible to elevate a relationship that has yet to be secured or solidified through agreement.

We understood this as children because when a boy liked a girl or vice versa, they would write on the note, "Will you go with me?" (I'm telling my age!) Then it would be accompanied with 'yes" and "no" boxes for the recipient to indicate their decision. In other words, agreement served as the precursor to relationship. "How can two walk together except they agree?" (Amos 3:3). When you attempt meaningful relationships in the absence of mutual agreement, it will result in either manipulation, frustration, or exhaustion.

Life-Sustaining Principle

When you attempt meaningful relationships in the absence of mutual agreement, it will result in either manipulation, frustration, or exhaustion.

John 1:11-13 (KJV)
He came unto his own, and his own received him not.
But as many as received him, to them gave he power to become the
sons of God, even to them that believe on his name: Which were

born, not of blood, nor of the will of the flesh, nor of the will of man, but of God.

Verse 11 states, Jesus came to His own and His own received Him not. The point we miss is this – He didn't force them to receive Him. The scripture goes on to say, But as many as received Him – to them He gave. There was no release of power until there was first agreement. Some of us have nothing to give to God because we are in relationships that are draining us dry due to the absence of agreement. They haven't received or accepted you, but you are continuously pouring into them. Employ wisdom by securing what is precious and waiting on the agreement.

Life-Sustaining Principle

Some of us have nothing to give to God because we are in relationships that are draining us dry due to the absence of agreement.

When you receive the cup of salvation, you come into agreement with God and His divine plan for your life. You accept the finished work of Jesus on the Cross. This decision lays the foundation for a deeper, more meaningful relationship to be developed. Then, you can transition into actively demonstrating your love towards Him through expressions of love. Needless to say, there are numerous expressions of love. Countless ways that we can show forth our love to the Father. Here in this chapter, I would like to highlight three and invite you to give them special consideration.

1st Expression of Love: Declarations

Jesus must be received. He must be welcomed. You must make a decision to invite Christ into your life. And then you must confess your decision. Romans 10:10 (KJV) states, "For with the heart man believeth unto righteousness, and with the mouth confession is made unto salvation."

Once we have a relationship with the Father and accept the sacrifice that Jesus made for us on the cross, one of the ways we can express our love is through the art of declaration. Just as communication is a vital aspect of our relationships with people, it is a vital aspect of our relationship with God. Our declarations provide us with an opportunity to show how much we love God. Here are just a few ways.

1. **Our declarations reveal to God that we are listening and taking His words to us seriously**. As a teacher, one of the ways I can check to see if someone heard and understood what I have communicated is to hear them verbalize those words back to me. As a minister of the gospel, I'm so blessed when weeks or years after delivering a sermon, someone can quote or share with me a major point they remember. Then, I know what was spoken reached and spoke to their spirit. When we

make declarations, we are not just talking. Spiritual declarations give voice to spiritual manifestations. Isaiah 55 verse 11 lets us know, "So shall my word be that goeth forth out of my mouth: it shall not return unto me void, but it shall accomplish that which I please, and it shall prosper in the thing whereto I sent it." Hear the Word, meditate on the Word, and then declare the word of God.

2. <u>**Our declarations reveal our level of agreement with what God has spoken**</u>. When we declare the promises of God, we are demonstrating our level of agreement with what God has spoken. Our declaration is a pronouncement of our faith. When God revealed to me that it was time for me to get married, as a single person dating no one, I begin to decree and declare that I was getting married. I didn't know to whom I would be married, and I didn't know when. But I knew what God had spoken concerning me, and I made the choice to declare my agreement. It took about a year and a half, and I was married. This is why daily declarations are so important. Each Sunday, at our local church, we take time out of the service to decree and to declare specific promises in the word of God.

3. <u>**Our declarations release the power of God to go to work on our behalf.**</u> Mark 11:23 (KJV) states, "For verily I say unto you, That whosoever shall say unto

this mountain, Be thou removed, and be thou cast into the sea; and shall not doubt in his heart, but shall believe that those things which he saith shall come to pass; he shall have whatsoever he saith". This scripture guarantees the believer that the power of God will accompany your declaration if you do not doubt in your heart.

4. **Our declarations birth establishments.** When God wanted a world, he spoke a word. We are created in the image of God. Job 22:28 (KJV) states, "Thou shalt also decree a thing, and it shall be established unto thee: and the light shall shine upon thy ways."

When we declare something, we are simply stating with authority what thus saith the Lord. In this case, we are specifically coming into agreement with what God has said to us and about us. When we open our mouths and express what God has spoken through His word or what God has shared with us through the Holy Spirit, the power of God is released. All the while, we are building and growing in our relationship with Jesus because we are honoring His word.

2nd Expression of Love: Offerings

Couched in the story of Gideon, is an exchange that magnifies how we can raise the level of our love expression towards God.

Judges 6:13-24 (KJV)

And Gideon said unto him, Oh my Lord, if the LORD be with us, why then is all this befallen us? and where be all his miracles which our fathers told us of, saying, Did not the LORD bring us up from Egypt? but now the LORD hath forsaken us, and delivered us into the hands of the Midianites. And the LORD looked upon him, and said, Go in this thy might, and thou shalt save Israel from the hand of the Midianites: have not I sent thee? And he said unto him, Oh my Lord, wherewith shall I save Israel? behold, my family is poor in Manasseh, and I am the least in my father's house. And the LORD said unto him, Surely I will be with thee, and thou shalt smite the Midianites as one man. And he said unto him, If now I have found grace in thy sight, then shew me a sign that thou talkest with me.

Depart not hence, I pray thee, until I come unto thee, and bring forth my present, and set it before thee. And he said, I will tarry until thou come again. And Gideon went in, and made ready a kid, and unleavened cakes of an ephah of flour: the flesh he put in a basket, and he put the broth in a pot, and brought it out unto him under the oak, and presented it. And the angel of God said unto him, Take the flesh and the unleavened cakes, and lay them upon this rock, and pour out the broth. And he did so. Then the angel of the LORD put forth the end of the staff that was in his hand, and touched the flesh and the unleavened cakes; and there rose up fire out of the rock, and consumed the flesh and the unleavened cakes. Then the angel of the LORD departed out of his sight. And when

Gideon perceived that he was an angel of the LORD, Gideon said, Alas, O LORD God! for because I have seen an angel of the LORD face to face. And the LORD said unto him, Peace be unto thee; fear not: thou shalt not die. Then Gideon built an altar there unto the LORD, and called it Jehovahshalom: unto this day it is yet in Ophrah of the Abiezrites.

The Angel of the Lord Waited

Gideon was being commissioned by an Angel to assume a leadership position in God's army. God was giving Him orders to smite the Midianites. Gideon, like most of us, was quite reluctant to answer the call and wanted to be sure that it was indeed the Lord who was speaking with him. The story has a predictable turn of events until we listen to the exchange between Gideon and the Angel of the Lord. Gideon asks the Angel, "please do not depart from me until I can bring you back a present (offering) and set it before you." And the Angel said, "I will wait here until you come back." Not only did the Angel wait, but once Gideon returned, the Angel told Gideon how to place the offering and then consumed the offering.

In the past, I have heard people minimize the giving of offerings unto the Lord. They say things like, "The church is all about money" or "All preachers want is your money." The fact that the Angel of the Lord waited for Gideon to go and prepare an offering symbolizes the significance that heaven places on how we express our love to God, specifically in offerings.

Your offering unto God is symbolic of your love for God. It should never be minimized or ruled as insignificant, even in times when we are experiencing lack or hardship. Here, I would like to highlight four things that your seed or offering to God should symbolize.

Your Sacrifice

Simply stated, the word sacrifice denotes offering something of meaningful significance to another. When we speak concerning offerings, I will speak in terms of money because it is the currency of our day. Yet, money is just one thing that we can sacrifice or offer to God. Some of us need to be more deliberate in sacrificing our time to God. The main point here is that we must ask ourselves, "What am I sacrificing unto God?". 'How am I expressing my love to God?" "What am I offering to God that is precious to me?" My time is very precious to me, but my Savior is more precious. What am I willing to sacrifice in my relationship with God? While "NOTHING" will match the value of what was sacrificed to us by God, "SOMETHING" must symbolize our acknowledgment that the sacrifice was made.

Your Substance

I know what it's like to sit in a church service and feel pressured to give. I think it's fair to say that God never intended his children to experience pressure when giving to him. I have also heard it said that you can't give what you do not have. As simple as this statement sounds, many people have given in offerings, only to experience a great deal of regret and anguish afterward. But, God loves a cheerful giver. And we must purpose to give of our substance.

Throughout your life, your actual substance will change. As your employment changes, as your streams of income vary, the substance that you have to draw upon will also change. So, how can you express your commitment towards God when your income is guaranteed to fluctuate throughout your lifetime. One way is to develop disciplines and purpose certain commitments regardless of varying circumstances. If you purpose to tithe 10% and give God an offering of 5%, this is a principle and a commitment that you exercise from employment to retirement. I know people that tithe 12% or 15%. I know that many Christians struggle with the concept of tithing, but I often tell people, tithing is the floor, not the ceiling. Tithing represents the least that we can offer to God, not the maximum. Those that purpose to exercise their faith on a higher level, give on a higher level. Consequently, they also receive at a higher level. Why? Because God ministers seed to the sower.

We should never give out of manipulation. Give unto God with a cheerful heart, setting aside at the beginning of the week, what you have purposed in your heart to give to God. Give of your substance. Give from what you have been given and give in faith believing that "God is able to make all grace abound toward you, that ye, always having all sufficiency in all things; may abound to every good work" (2 Corinthians 9:8).

Your Steadfastness

Thirdly, your offering should be symbolic of your steadfastness or consistency with God. I purpose in my heart to offer a tithe and an offering to God on a consistent basis. When we're in love relationships, consistency is a major point of evaluation. If someone is only randomly concerned or randomly expressive towards us, we don't have as much confidence in their love towards us. Why? Because their love expressions lack consistency. Are you randomly expressing your love to God, or have you purposed in your heart to express your love in purposeful, meaningful, and consistent ways? Gideon asked the Angel to wait, and then he ran and prepared an offering. It demonstrated that he had a heart for wanting to express back to God his love and appreciation for him. It further demonstrated that he was familiar with pulling together an offering for the Lord. He made haste to do what had been done before.

Your Spiritual Maturity

When we are babies, we absorb everybody's love and attention. When we are babies, we have no obligation to offer anything back to those that are lavishing us with love. A grin here, a smile there, will prove to be more than sufficient for doting parents and grandparents. But, as we get older, the expectations change. I expect my 12-year-old daughter to say thank you when I go out of my way to get her something special. Further, I expect her to be more than willing to contribute to the needs of the house and not constantly remain on the receiving end. As she matures, I expect her maturity to be evident in her love expressions towards her father and me.

As we mature in God, our love expressions should also mature. We should ask the question, "God, how can I love you better?" And then wait for the answer. Take notes on the answer. Then endeavor to rise to the occasion.

3ʳᵈ Expression of Love: Altars

Judges 6: 22-24
And when Gideon perceived that he was an angel of the LORD, Gideon said, Alas, O LORD God! for because I have seen an angel of the LORD face to face. And the LORD said unto him, Peace be unto thee; fear not: thou shalt not die. Then Gideon built an altar there unto the LORD, and called it Jehovahshalom: unto this day it is yet in Ophrah of the Abiezrites.

Why Build An Altar?

We can learn a great deal from Gideon's call and commission by God. Not only did Gideon ask the Angel to wait, so that he could prepare an offering. He also decided to construct an altar. Again, as we examine Gideon's response to his divine visitation, we see clearly yet another way that we can immediately heighten our love expression towards God – build an altar.

One could easily argue that anywhere God chooses to meet you or visit you, forever denotes that place as a holy or sacred place. Moses, take off your shoes, for the ground that you are standing on, is holy ground. The place was common and familiar to Moses. But the day God decided to meet him there, that place became a holy place. Gideon knew that he had just experienced a divine visitation that would forever "mark" his life and his ministry. He experienced an identity shift, and he would never be able to return to the erroneous way he viewed himself. More importantly, he had just experienced a divine encounter with the almighty God.

Creating an altar is one way to mark or denote a significant change or shift has occurred in your life. Divine encounters should never be treated haphazardly or as insignificant, no matter how frequently they may occur. When the believer creates an altar, they mark the moment that everything changed in the spirit realm.

A modern-day altar can also serve as a place that you have designated and set aside to meet God. Sometimes, it's a corner in a closet with a blanket, a Bible, and a few scriptures on the wall. Sometimes it's a room that you enter that you have consecrated as a holy place. The reality is – sometimes it's your car. Here's one thing that I have learned. God will honor the place that you consecrate as sacred unto Him.

I remember when I moved away from home for the first time. I moved over 5 hours away and unfortunately, I had limited furniture and resources. For the initial 4 to 6 months in my apartment, I had a small sleeper sofa and an old, worn recliner chair. The recliner chair became my sacred place for my special time with God. I would kneel in front of the chair and pray. Or I would climb into the chair and pray. I can honestly say that God met me at that chair. That's been over 20 years ago and now I have a room where I go to spend time with God. I share this with you so that you realize, it matters not how great or how small the altar is that you set up as a consecrated space to meet God. What matters is that you create one. What matters is that you carve out space to meet and commune with your Creator.

Judges 6:24 NIV

So Gideon built an altar to the Lord there and called it The Lord Is Peace. To this day it stands in Ophrah of the Abiezrites.

Gideon called the altar Jehovah-shalom, meaning The Lord is Peace. Altars and divine encounters establish for us divine places of peace. We are living in a world where so many, young and old, are devoid of peace. Establishing a place where we step aside from the noise of this world and set our mind and affections on things that are above and not below – ushers us to a place of peace that the world and people cannot disrupt. We have peace even when we are preparing for life's most serious battles.

Are you ready to express your love to God in a way that grasps the Father's attention? When we mature in Christ, we are no longer babes seeking only what we can <u>receive</u>. Instead, we are seeking for ways that we can love God better. We are seeking for ways to cultivate a level of intimacy with Him that we have with no one else. In this chapter, I have provided you with just three love expressions that you can employ to further enhance and develop your love relationship with the Father.

Questions:

1. Take a moment to think about your relationship with God. What do you believe you are doing well? What are some things that you could do better?

_____

_____

_____

_____

2. What are three scripturally based declarations that you can incorporate into your daily confessions?

_____

_____

_____

_____

_____

3. What are some scripturally based declarations you can declare over your children, family and/or loved ones?

_____

_____

_____

_____

4. When you reflect on offerings, what have you purposed in your heart to give to God as an offering?

    _____

    _____

    _____

    _____

5. Think about at least 3 life changing moments when you know God intervened on your behalf. Use the space below to record those times. Have you shared with anyone recently about what God has done for you?

    _____

    _____

    _____

    _____

6. What are some practical ways that we as Christians today can build altars unto God?

    _____

    _____

    _____

    _____

7. Do you have a prayer room or prayer closet in your home? Talk about some of the creative spaces where you purpose to meet God.

_____

_____

_____

_____

Chapter 7

Becoming a Game Changer
Through Obedience
by Gary Becton

Study Scriptures: Judges 6:25-31 KJV

> [25] And it came to pass the same night, that the LORD said unto him, Take thy father's young bullock, even the second bullock of seven years old, and throw down the altar of Baal that thy father hath, and cut down the grove that is by it: [26] And build an altar unto the LORD thy God upon the top of this rock, in the ordered place, and take the second bullock, and offer a burnt sacrifice with the wood of the grove which thou shalt cut down. [27] Then Gideon took ten men of his servants, and did as the LORD had said unto him: and so it was, because he feared his father's household, and the men of the city, that he could not do it by day, that he did it by night. [28] And when the men of the city arose early in the morning, behold, the altar of Baal was cast down, and the grove was cut down that was by it, and the second bullock was offered upon the altar that was built. [29] And they said one to another, Who hath done this thing? And when they enquired and asked, they said, Gideon the son of Joash hath done this thing. [30] Then the men of the city said unto Joash, Bring out thy son, that he may die: because he hath cast down the altar of Baal, and because he hath cut down the grove that was by it. [31] And Joash said unto all that stood against him, Will ye plead for Baal? will ye save him? he that will plead for him, let him be put to death whilst it is yet morning: if he be a god, let him plead for himself, because one hath cast down his altar.

Prayer:

To the Alpha and Omega, the Beginning and the End, my Father, Creator of heaven and earth. Lord, I come before you in prayer through Jesus Christ, my Lord, and Savior. Father, I thank you for the Holy Spirit. I thank you for the wisdom, knowledge, and understanding that you will allow to flow off the pages of this book that is written to bring you glory, honor, and praise. Father, for those reading this book, may it be a spiritual awakening that will increase their relationship with you in the realm of obedience to the Trinity. Holy Spirit, I call upon you to flow through me like rivers of living water, while you write this chapter to release supernatural gifts of the spirit into the hearts and minds of those who will read this book. I pray that they are equipped to produce results of victory, authority, and the power of God in the earth realm.

In Jesus Name, I pray,

Amen.

Gideon, a man of God and a prophet of God, was called into service because of the disobedience of God's chosen people the Israelites. Gideon was obedient to God's words. I understand now, when the word of God says, "If ye love me, keep my commandments" (John 14:15 KJV). You and I have been released upon the earth to love God, and we do this by keeping God's commandments.

God knew he could trust Gideon, so he called Gideon into action, just like God is calling you and me into action; specifically, the act of obedience. The rebelliousness of the Israelites required God to teach them a lesson. Sometimes in our disobedience, we fail to think about how we have hurt God or how we have grieved the Holy Spirit. I can only imagine that God has feelings; God has a heart. I say this because He created you and I in His image. If I have a heart, if I have feelings, then surely my Father in heaven has them too.

God is a God of purpose, plan, and design. God's purpose is to restore the Kingdom of heaven back to the earth. His plan is for mankind to be the bridge to allow the Kingdom of God (in heaven) to be released upon the earth (Mathew 6:9 -13). His design can be seen in the wonderful uniqueness of His children. God wants to use us to accomplish His will in the earth. Yet, even in our uniqueness, God has not removed the element of choice and free-will.

Deuteronomy 30:15-16 (NLT)

Now listen! Today I am giving you a choice between life and death, between prosperity and disaster. For I command you this day to love the Lord your God and to keep his commands, decrees, and regulations by walking in his ways. If you do this, you will live and multiply, and the Lord your God will bless you and the land you are about to enter and occupy.

One Word: Obedience

As you pursue your identity in the Kingdom, understand that obedience is everything! The key to unlocking the wisdom, assurance, and protection you need to fulfill your assignment is through your faith and your obedience to carry out God's instructions. We will deal with faith in the next chapter. But, this chapter is focused on obedience. In order to please God, Gideon had to go against the grain of the world's system. Are you prepared to go against the grain of the world's system? The world's system has driven mankind to put all of his energy and focus into working hard to make a dollar in order to purchase cars, houses, land and various kinds of materialistic goods. Once these things are acquired, a person is considered "successful". Yet, he or she often has to work around the clock to maintain the "success" gained within the world's system. The Word of God admonishes us in Matthew 6:33, "But seek ye first the kingdom of God, and his righteousness, and all these things shall be added unto you." Success in the Kingdom of God does not equate to the accumulation of things. It equates to a quality of life that allows us to walk in Kingdom authority to be fruitful, multiply and replenish the earth. Success in the Kingdom of God bears little resemblance to success in the world's system. In order to really become a Game Changer through obedience, you must be willing to challenge and re-examine your definition of success.

Life-Sustaining Principle

The key to unlocking the wisdom, assurance, and protection you need to fulfill your assignment is through your faith and your obedience to carry out God's instructions.

Slaying His Father's Demons

Judges 6: 25-26

Here in this text, Gideon was commanded to destroy or throw down one of his father's prized possessions – his altar of Baal – along with the Asherah pole standing beside it. It is very important to understand that when Joash, Gideon's father, was instructed by God not to worship false gods, out of his disobedience Joash opened the door for generational curses to follow his bloodline. It would have been easy for Gideon to follow in his father's footsteps and allow this curse to continue. But Gideon desired to please the God of heaven and earth. Gideon had to make his own choice as a man; a choice to serve and obey God or a choice to please his natural father. Before Gideon would be tasked with fighting an external enemy, he would first have to confront the demons plaguing his own family. In all things, God is a God of order. Some believers are attempting to fight spiritual battles in the world but overlooking the demonic activity that's attacking their own bloodline. Often times, this demonic activity has gained access through open doors of disobedience.

Life-Sustaining Principle

Some believers are attempting to fight spiritual battles in the world but overlooking the demonic activity that's attacking their own bloodline. Often times, this demonic activity has gained access through open doors of disobedience.

Gideon was a Game Changer. Game Changers are people that go against the religious order and the world's system in order to tap into the supernatural power of God through obedience, prayer, and intimate relationship with the Father, Son, and Holy Spirit. Game Changers desire to see the power of God. The power that was displayed in the book of Acts. For years, people have been "preached to", but Game Changers don't just preach or teach the Word of God, they serve as examples of God's Word of Power. In this time and season, God is pouring out more of His Spirit on those Game Changers that seek after Him.

Life-Sustaining Principle

Game Changers are people that go against the religious order and the world's system in order to tap into the supernatural power of God through obedience, prayer, and intimate relationship with the Father, Son, and Holy Spirit.

A Game Changer Within the Family

God is calling many of us to serve as Game Changers within our family's *first*. Our loyalty to God must supersede our loyalty to all others. This includes parents, siblings, friends, coworkers and even church members. Our loyalty and obedience must be unto God and His Word. In order to stand as a Game Changer as it relates to your natural family, there are three essential tests that you will have to successfully pass.

The Test of Rejection

When Gideon chose to be obedient to God, he knew that he was also risking the rejection of his family. Specifically, the rejection of his father. Sometimes the very act of obedience God is calling us to is in direct opposition to the beliefs, traditions, or practices of our family. Gideon had to dismantle his father's idol. We often hear about peer pressure, but sometimes we are challenged with family pressure. When examining the life of Jesus, the Bible lets us know that He came to His own and His own received Him not (John 1:11). In essence, He was rejected by those that were closest to Him. To serve as a Game Changer within your Family, you will have to weather seasons of rejection without giving in to the pressure to abandon your faith. This is key to walking in your Kingdom identity. Our Kingdom identity must be rooted and grounded in the will of God for our lives, not the will of our families or the pressures of the world's system.

Life-Sustaining Principle

Our Kingdom identity must be rooted and grounded in the will of God for our lives, not the will of our families or the pressures of the world's system.

When you are rejected by your family or a close circle of friends, it is important to realize that although you have been rejected, you are probably being closely watched. People closest to you want to know if you are serious. So, they will watch to see if you adhere to your own personal convictions. They will search your life to identify any hypocritical tendencies or behaviors. It's during this time that it's important that you remain steadfast in your personal convictions. It's never wise to portray ourselves as perfect or inhuman, but we should also demonstrate a seriousness regarding our walk with God.

The Test of Reconstruction

The second test is the test of reconstruction. It is important to note that even in our obedience to God, God is not commissioning us to *just* tear down. The Bible says that God ordered Gideon to tear down his father's idol, but he also instructed Gideon to build the proper kind of altar. Religious minded people tear down with no plan to build or reconstruct. Kingdom Warriors understand the importance of building and establishing what is proper in the place of what has been destroyed. Often times, when it comes to spiritual correction with family members and close friends, we are quick to tear down, but we're not as diligent when it comes to building. If God is calling you to dismantle a tradition, belief, or behavior in your family, God will give you the wisdom of what to build in its place.

Life-Sustaining Principle

Often times, when it comes to family members and close friends, we are eager to tear down, but not as diligent when it comes to building. If God is calling you to dismantle a tradition, belief, or behavior in your family, God will give you the wisdom of what to build in its place.

The Test of Reconnection

Inevitably, more often than not, family members, once they understand that you are not changing your mind, will want to reconnect. They might reach out to you in a time of need for prayer or assistance. This is an awesome time to demonstrate the love of Christ as opposed to giving them an "I Told You So" speech. Demonstrating the love of Christ in the reconnection is essential. Game Changers demonstrate the love of Christ because that's Kingdom. It's Kingdom love and Kingdom obedience.

Let's look at how Gideon's courage caused a higher or deeper connection with his father.

Judges 6: 28-32

And when the men of the city arose early in the morning, behold, the altar of Baal was cast down, and the grove was cut down that was by it, and the second bullock was offered upon the altar that was built. And they said one to another, Who hath done this thing? And when they enquired and asked, they said, Gideon the son of Joash hath done this thing. Then the men of the city said unto Joash, Bring out thy son, that he may die: because he hath cast down the altar of Baal, and because he hath cut down the grove that was by it. And Joash said unto all that stood against him, Will ye plead for Baal? will ye save him? he that will plead for him, let him be put to death whilst it is yet morning: if he be a god, let him plead for himself, because one hath cast down his altar. Therefore on that day he called him Jerubbaal, saying, Let Baal plead against him, because he hath thrown down his altar.

By operating in obedience and dealing with his father's idol, Gideon immediately stopped the generational curse of idol worship. Think about that. He utterly destroyed an idol that his father refused to conquer. You would think that Joash would have been angry and moved to go against his son for tearing down his altar. You would think that Joash would agree with the people for fear that the people would strike him down and attempt to kill his son. But Joash stood with compassion and wisdom. He stood in courage once he realized his son's act of courage.

I believe God touched Joash's heart and gave him the wisdom to stand against the people and the idol that he himself lacked the strength to tear down. Gideon's act of obedience to God was a game-changer for Israel and for his father Joash. Grace and mercy were extended to Gideon's father because of the obedience of his son. There are times when our obedience to God serves as a form of intercession for other generations. This is why it is so important that we rise to the level of obedience to God. There are literally lives at stake.

Obedience Doesn't Always Mean the Absence of Fear

Enduring this level of testing is not going to be easy, but Game Changers chase after the mind of Christ and the heart of Christ. In following God's instructions, the enemy will always send the spirit of fear to attempt to influence you to disobey God's instructions. Obedience to God does not mean the complete absence of fear. As believers, we sometimes underestimate the amount of progress we can make even in fearful moments. Gideon was fearful of being killed by Joash and the Israelites that followed the false god Baal. His fear caused him to make moves in the darkness, but his fear did not render him paralyzed to God's instructions. Gideon pushed back fear and moved in the wisdom of God. He gathered ten men - men whom he could trust, who would stand with him and have his back to help him follow God's instructions. When you move in obedience to God's instructions, He will empower you with everything you need to get the job done.

Understanding the Process

Once you fully understand your Kingdom identity, it elevates you to walk in the spirit of obedience. That elevation and consistency over time produces Kingdom integrity. Kingdom integrity is a consistent lifestyle of obedience to the Holy Spirit which allows you to operate in victory in natural as well as supernatural realms. This allows the Kingdom of Heaven to flow through you so that the perfect will of God is released upon the Earth. This is also why you must understand your identity and know who you are and whose you are. Once you understand that you are a child of the King, you live according to the King's rules. You live to please the King. Game Changers live in this realm- the realm of obedience. Abiding in this realm of obedience produces this Kingdom lifestyle and mindset. It is a lifestyle that is marked by love, authority, power and integrity. The Holy Spirit helps us in this process by bringing forth warnings, clarity, and direction when needed. Allowing you to access your Kingdom inheritance.

Life-Sustaining Principle

Kingdom integrity is a consistent lifestyle of obedience to the Holy Spirit which allows you to operate in victory in natural as well as supernatural realms.

The world's system that we live in today attempts to condition our minds to think that in order to be successful we have to have achieved a higher education, we have to have a house and a car. We have to be married and have children. These things make you successful in the world's system. The world's system will require you to depend on the world. God's system will require you to depend on God and His promises. God's system according to Matthew 6:33 KJV states, "But seek ye first the kingdom of God, and his righteousness; and all these things shall be added unto you." Here, we have two different systems. God's system is the system that produces that Kingdom inheritance.

Game Changer Status

Walking in your Kingdom inheritance makes you a Game Changer on many levels. Game Changer status will release a Kingdom quality of life and favor on you and your blood line for generations to come. Proverbs 20:7 states "The just man walketh in his integrity: his children are blessed after him." Game Changers will turn the world upside down as the Apostles and believers of the way did in the New Testament. As Romans 14:11b KJV lets us know, "...every knee will bow to me, and every tongue shall confess to God."

When I think about Game Changers, I think about my great grandmother Betsy. Although she is no longer with us, I remember how mighty the hand of God was upon her life. I witnessed my great grandmother talk to a drunken man and he became sober. I saw my great grandmother move in faith when we traveled on bald tires in the snow from North Carolina to Richmond, Virginia to get my father out of jail over the weekend. Although we didn't have money for a hotel and just enough gas to get to Richmond, Virginia, my great grandmother called those things that be not as though they were.

As a result of her faith, strangers in Richmond, Virginia offered their home to us and fed us like kings and queens. They responded to us after seeing us parked on the side of the road sleeping in the car. When we prepared to leave, this family also gave my great grandmother money to return home. Once my great grandmother arrived at the jail, she was also able to get my father released. This was indeed a miracle as during this time a black man arrested in Virginia was not getting out of jail over the weekend.

In watching my great grandmother as a Game Changer, it influenced my life and caused me to desire the anointing that was on her life. As a child, she spoke into my life that I would one day become a preacher. Looking back on it now, I realize that my great grandmother was a prophet and that same anointing is upon me. My great grandmother Betsy was a Game Changer and she influenced generations.

Characteristics of a Game Changer

God is calling you to be a Game Changer for the Kingdom of God. With one act of obedience, Gideon changed the game for his bloodline and for a generation of people. We are in a season now when God is raising up men and women of God willing to impact another generation. As we close this chapter, I would like to identify 7 key characteristics of Game Changers.

1.   Game Changers are Glory Carriers.

Colossians 1:27-29 KJV
To whom God would make known what is the riches of the glory of this mystery among the Gentiles; which is Christ in you, the hope of glory: Whom we preach, warning every man, and teaching every man in all wisdom; that we may present every man perfect in Christ Jesus: Whereunto I also labour, striving according to his working, which worketh in me mightily.

Ephesians 3:14-21 King James Version (KJV)
For this cause I bow my knees unto the Father of our Lord Jesus Christ, Of whom the whole family in heaven and earth is named, That he would grant you, according to the riches of his glory, to be strengthened with might by his Spirit in the inner man; That Christ may dwell in your hearts by faith; that ye, being rooted and grounded in love, May be able to comprehend with all saints what is the breadth, and length, and depth, and height; And to know the love of Christ, which passeth knowledge, that ye might be filled with all the fulness of God. Now unto him that is able to do exceeding abundantly above all that we ask or think, according to the power that worketh in us, Unto him be glory in the church by Christ Jesus throughout all ages, world without end. Amen.

2.   Game Changers allow themselves to be purged.

Malachi 3:22-23 King James Version (KJV)

But who may abide the day of his coming? and who shall stand when he appeareth? for he is like a refiner's fire, and like fullers' soap: And he shall sit as a refiner and purifier of silver: and he shall purify the sons of Levi, and purge them as gold and silver, that they may offer unto the LORD an offering in righteousness.

2 Corinthians 7:1 King James Version (KJV)

Having therefore these promises, dearly beloved, let us cleanse ourselves from all filthiness of the flesh and spirit, perfecting holiness in the fear of God.

3.   Game Changers understand that there will be times when they will walk alone because the natural-minded man does not understand the things of God.

1 Corinthians 2:9-14 King James Version (KJV)

But as it is written, Eye hath not seen, nor ear heard, neither have entered into the heart of man, the things which God hath prepared for them that love him. But God hath revealed them unto us by his Spirit: for the Spirit searcheth all things, yea, the deep things of God. For what man knoweth the things of a man, save the spirit of man which is in him? even so the things of God knoweth no man, but the Spirit of God. Now we have received, not the spirit of the world, but the spirit which is of God; that we might know the things that are freely given to us of God. Which things also we speak, not in the words which man's wisdom teacheth, but which the Holy Ghost teacheth; comparing spiritual things with spiritual. But the natural man receiveth not the things of the Spirit of God: for they are foolishness unto him: neither can he know them, because they are spiritually discerned.

4. Game Changers understand the power and significance of obedience.

Hebrews 5:8 King James Version (KJV)
Though he were a Son, yet learned he obedience by the things which he suffered; And being made perfect, he became the author of eternal salvation for all who obey him, Called of God an high priest after the order of Melchizedek.

5. Game Changers are willing to turn away from the world's system.

Matthew 6:24 King James Version (KJV)
No man can serve two masters: for either he will hate the one, and love the other; or else he will hold to the one, and despise the other. Ye cannot serve God and mammon.

6. Game Changers know how to act out their responsibilities towards God.

Philippians 2:13 (KJV)
For it is God which worketh in you both to will and to do of his good pleasure.

7. Game Changers are willing to keep their eyes fixed on Jesus Christ.

Hebrews 12:1-2 (KJV)

Wherefore seeing we also are compassed about with so great a cloud of witnesses, let us lay aside every weight, and the sin which doth so easily beset us, and let us run with patience the race that is set before us, Looking unto Jesus the author and finisher of our faith; who for the joy that was set before him endured the cross, despising the shame, and is set down at the right hand of the throne of God.

God's perfect will for our life is to be a Game Changer in obedience to His Word, presenting our bodies unto Him, not as unto the world. Game Changers endeavor to live holy lives, yielding to the Father, Son, and Holy Spirit in order to prove what is the good, acceptable, and perfect will of God; living in the realm of natural and supernatural, allowing the Kingdom of God to flow on earth as it is in heaven.

Jesus said in Matthew 6:9-13 KJV, "After this manner therefore pray ye: Our Father which art in heaven, Hallowed be thy name. Thy kingdom come, Thy will be done in earth, as it is in heaven. Give us this day our daily bread. And forgive us our debts, as we forgive our debtors. And lead us not into temptation, but deliver us from evil: For thine is the kingdom, and the power, and the glory, forever. Amen."

Questions

1. Create a definition for the word "success" that you can use as you move forward in your Kingdom identity?

   _____

   _____

   _____

   _____

2. When was the last time you had to hold on to your personal convictions in the midst of pressure from family or close friends? How did you handle it?

   _____

   _____

   _____

   _____

3. Why is it dangerous or unwise to dismantle a tradition, belief, or behavior in your family, without seeking God for the wisdom of what to build in its place?

   _____

   _____

   _____

   _____

4. How was Gideon's act of courage a form of intercession for his father?

_____

_____

_____

_____

5. When might it be wise to make "faith moves" in the dark?

_____

_____

_____

_____

6. In what ways do you see the Spirit of the Lord using you to serve as a Game Changer in your family, your church or in the world?

_____

_____

_____

_____

7. As you think about your family, who has been a Game Changer as it relates to your blood line? Why?

_____

_____

_____

_____

_____

_____

8. Reflect on your personal walk with God, how can you be the Game Changer that generations after you will one day hold in high regard?

_____

_____

_____

_____

_____

_____

Chapter 8
Arriving at a Place of Spiritual Maturity
by Shawn Moreland and Kylie McBride

Scripture: Judges 6:34-40 KJV

---

³⁴ But the Spirit of the LORD came upon Gideon, and he blew a trumpet; and Abiezer was gathered after him. ³⁵ And he sent messengers throughout all Manasseh; who also was gathered after him: and he sent messengers unto Asher, and unto Zebulun, and unto Naphtali; and they came up to meet them. ³⁶ And Gideon said unto God, If thou wilt save Israel by mine hand, as thou hast said, ³⁷ Behold, I will put a fleece of wool in the floor; and if the dew be on the fleece only, and it be dry upon all the earth beside, then shall I know that thou wilt save Israel by mine hand, as thou hast said. ³⁸ And it was so: for he rose up early on the morrow, and thrust the fleece together, and wringed the dew out of the fleece, a bowl full of water. ³⁹ And Gideon said unto God, Let not thine anger be hot against me, and I will speak but this once: let me prove, I pray thee, but this once with the fleece; let it now be dry only upon the fleece, and upon all the ground let there be dew. ⁴⁰ And God did so that night: for it was dry upon the fleece only, and there was dew on all the ground.

Prayer

Father, I believe, but I ask that you help my unbelief. Open my blinded eyes that I may see beyond what is immediately in front of me. Please forgive me when I'm unsure, and my faith is wavering. Help me to trust in your word, as you lead and guide me into victory. Help me to mature in my faith. In you, my God, I trust.
In Jesus Name,
Amen.

When the Call of God is Simply Hard to Believe

Gideon was told by God that God was going to use him to rescue Israel. At first, Gideon's warrior mentality and liberative instinct motivated him to call out for help from other tribes. He called for the Abiezrites to follow him. He also sent messengers throughout Manasseh, Asher, Zebulun, and Nephtali. In other words, he sent for people he trusted to fight along with him. He appeared ready for the battle. Then something happened. His faith was interrupted.

In the heat of the moment, Gideon allowed a sense of doubt and fear to settle into his mind and spirit. My guess is we've all been there when we: 1) doubt whether or not we have heard the voice of God, or 2) doubt if we really have a clear revelation or understanding regarding God's timing. When trying to manage these contradicting and sometimes invasive thoughts, fear can become the manager of our emotions. We see this in the story of Peter when he walked out unto the water, Peter conquered the impossible as long as his eyes remained fixed on Jesus. Once Peter took his eyes off of Jesus, he began to sink. Gideon took his eyes off God for a brief moment and began to doubt that God was going to be with him through his impending journey. Gideon's lack of assurance caused him to doubt and waver in trusting that God would indeed use him to save the Israelites.

Have you ever looked at a picture of yourself and said, "I can't believe that's me!!!" You look more beautiful or handsome than you could have ever imagined. Sometimes we have a similar experience when we examine the calling of God on our lives. There are times when it is simply "unbelievable." As a matter of fact, most of the time, the calling of God on our lives is simply unbelievable *to us*. We just don't quite see ourselves in that particular way. The reality is, if your calling is easy to embrace, then mature faith would not be required.

Why is it often hard to believe what God has called us to do? The truth is, we *know* ourselves. Our frailties, our insecurities, our failures, even our indiscretions. Consequently, when we begin to more fully understand what God is calling us to do, we immediately begin to focus on our shortcomings and insufficiencies. We keep a record of our personal failures while God has already thrown them into the sea of forgetfulness (Micah 7:4). We allow past mistakes and even present struggles to frustrate what God is endeavoring to do in and through us. When we allow our past failures or present struggles to conquer our thinking, we glorify those things more than the great creator God. We must trust that if God calls us and gives us a plan, God will see us through. God is not like man. His faithfulness is a non-negotiable.

Life-Sustaining Principle

Sometimes the calling of God on our lives is simply "unbelievable"... If your calling is easy to embrace, then mature faith would not be required.

Another mindset that causes doubt and fear to surface concerning the call of God is the wayward thinking that says, "I'm not good enough or holy enough." Sometimes, this feeling is due to leaders who lack a certain level of transparency or who have not been completely honest about their own shortcomings. Couple this with the fact that the enemy desires for us to be more sin-conscious than grace-conscious and you will begin to understand the war that tends to go on in the minds of many believers. Focusing more on our insufficiencies and insecurities directs us in the opposite direction of grace, and grace is the whole message of Jesus Christ. Ephesians 2:8-9 (KJV) states, "For by grace are ye saved through faith; and that not of yourselves: it is the gift of God: Not of works, lest any man should boast." There is nothing we can do in our flesh to warrant salvation or the grace that accompanies it. Therefore, Jesus became sin so that we can become righteous, completing the redemptive work of the Father. The gift of His life is a perpetual testimony of grace at work.

When There Are More Questions Than Answers

Because the call of God was difficult to believe, Gideon started questioning God. Tradition says that we should not question God. However, questioning God is not the problem; it is

140

the attitude with which the question is posed that can cause a problem. We are never to indict God; to do so would be extremely reckless. It is, however, permissible to approach Him with honest questions. He is, after all, the originator of all knowledge, wisdom, and understanding. As we strive to find clarity regarding God's plan for our lives, dialogue with God is essential. During those times of intimate conversation with the Father, be confident that God's ear is inclined to your cry – even if your cry is being articulated as a question. Because He desires for us to have clarity, He will indeed respond.

Gideon asked God to send him a sign to confirm that God would be with him as he led an army to confront and conquer their enemy. We can see that Gideon's relationship with God is one that is quite intimate; so much so that he was able to communicate with God about his insecurity and lack of confidence. What is striking is that God listens, but He does not allow Gideon to forgo the assignment.

Life-Sustaining Principle

God knows that there are times when we feel insecure or lack the confidence needed to answer the call of God.

In Judges 6 verses 36 and 37, Gideon questioned God: "And Gideon said unto God, if thou wilt save Israel by mine hand, as thou has said, Behold, I will put a fleece of wool in the floor; and if the dew be on the fleece only, and it be dry upon all the earth beside, then shall I know that thou wilt save Israel by mine hand, as thou hast said."

"Growing Up" in Our Faith

Isn't this what we say to God, if you are *really* going to use me or if you are *really* going to fulfill this specific promise, prove it to me in this particular way. We begin to present God with challenges to test and see if God is really going to show up and prove himself by doing the things that He already said He would do. Hebrews 11:1 (KJV) tells us, "Now faith is the substance of things hoped for, the evidence of things not seen." Our faith is supposed to produce the evidence, but when our faith is immature, we ask God to produce the evidence. In Judges 6 verses 37 and 38, Gideon said "I will put a wool fleece on the threshing floor tonight. If the fleece is wet with dew in the morning, but the ground is dry, then I will know that you are going to help me rescue Israel as you promised." When Gideon got up early the next morning, he squeezed the fleece and wrung out a whole bowl full of water. This is what we have to do with the fear that is attempting to saturate our hearts and minds. We must rid ourselves of doubt and fear. It is imperative that we *squeeze out* fear, allowing it to occupy no space in our lives. Fear and faith cannot co-exist; one must make way for the other.

Life-Sustaining Principle

Our faith is supposed to produce the evidence, but when our faith is immature, we ask God to produce the evidence.

The Bible is filled with many examples of men and women who asked God to produce the evidence. Let's take Moses, for example. Faced with the task of leading a rebellious people through hostile territory and into the Promised Land, Moses asked God to make Himself visible before he could feel confident that He was with him on the journey through the wilderness (Exodus 33:18-20). Truthfully, Moses had already experienced many infallible pieces of evidence of God's presence, but he asked for an additional confirmation concerning the call of God on his life. A loving and understanding God obliged him. Or we can take the story of the priest Zechariah in Luke 1. The angel appeared to Zechariah after years of him requesting a child to assure him that his prayers were about to be answered. However, Zechariah, the priest, answers (Luke 1:18 KJV), "...Whereby shall I know this? for I am an old man, and my wife well stricken in years". Zechariah is actually asking this question of the angel that came to deliver the news. As a result, the angel shares with Zechariah that he will be silent until the baby is born. God will sometimes command silence from you as a way of safeguarding His promise and not allowing it to be drowned with words of doubt or disbelief. Again, immature faith asks God to produce more evidence before you can believe.

Despite the many examples where God was prompted for "more" evidence, there are other examples where men and women simply took God at his Word. In Mark 10:46-52, the story is told of how blind Bartimaeus could not see, yet he believed the son of God would heal him just from him simply asking for his sight. Or we have the story of Mary, the mother of Jesus, who after hearing the salutation of the angel said in Luke 1:38, "...be it unto me according to thy word." Mature faith utilizes God's Word as all the evidence that is needed. Mature faith recognizes that God's Word is, in fact, the greatest evidence that an eternal God can offer. Isaiah 55:11 (KJV) states, "So shall my word be that goeth forth out of my mouth: it shall not return unto me void, but it shall accomplish that which I please, and it shall prosper in the thing whereto I sent it."

As the Word offers examples on both ends of the spectrum, the believer must be honest about their position of faith when petitioning God for additional 'evidence'. The use of the generality – fleecing God – does not speak to the varying perspective from which individuals approach God. Some will use this method in an effort to manipulate God and nullify His Word concerning them, in search of a loophole or private detour. I have been guilty of this in the past; asking God to perform ridiculous feats, such as allowing me to drive all the way to work without being stopped by any red lights, if it is His will that I do so and so. PSA: God is not in the red-light business, nor will He play those games. My request was connected to my unbelief and disobedience rather than an authentic desire to do what God was requiring. Gideon requested that God demonstrate the authenticity of the assignment, not because He did not believe God, but because he did not believe in the God in him. His request was not rooted in manipulation or an attempt the sidestep the assignment. God's promise to deliver Israel from oppression was one with which Gideon was very familiar. His resort to the angel signifies the history of God's miracle-working power on their behalf. Thus, the place of uncertainty was not concerning God's ability or timing, but His chosen leader. The implicit impetus for Gideon's multiple requests for further confirmation was a need for confirmation that God was absolutely sure that he was indeed the man for the job. God does not become disgruntled at our request for confirmation. The standard of 2 or 3 witnesses is presented throughout the scripture. Confirmation for the purpose of motivation is permissible in the sight of God. Manipulation for the purpose of dereliction breeds separation from the will and abortion of the assignment of God concerning you. Therefore, we approach God seeking confirmation as we prepare to do the will of the Father and not in a spirit of manipulation seeking to follow our own way.

Life-Sustaining Principle

God will sometimes command silence from you as a way of safeguarding His promise and not allowing it to be drowned with words of doubt or disbelief.

It was not until God proved himself to Gideon the second time that Gideon's faith was secure or matured. What is going to be required for you to become mature in your faith? Blind Bartimaeus was just a blind man begging by the side of the road. He heard that Jesus was in his vicinity, and he had enough faith to ask him to restore his sight because he knew that the son of The Lord could perform glorious works of God. After Bartimaeus asked for his sight to be restored to him, Jesus sent him on his way saying "...Go thy way; thy faith hath made thee whole. And immediately, he received his sight, and followed Jesus in the way (Mark 10:52 KJV)." Immediately, his sight was restored based on the strength of his faith. However, Gideon asked God to prove himself once, which he did, but his faith in God was still not solid. God allowed Gideon to fleece him a second time, after which, Gideon finally believed. Many have judged Gideon harshly, but his response was that of a natural man looking for supernatural assurance. Yet, when we remind ourselves on a daily basis that we too are supernatural beings, it will become much easier to believe a supernatural God.

Having Strong Faith Exhibits Trust in God, Even Without the Details

A real-life experience that explains how following and trusting God's plan without seeing all the details was when I transitioned from my old life in Trenton, New Jersey to a new unknown life in Columbia, South Carolina. I moved and found myself without employment but trusting that God would provide.

As my daughter and I were seeking employment, God provided us with all of our necessities. After a few months, things in our lives started changing, and we began to experience some difficult challenges. In the midst of adjusting to a new environment and being faced with new trials, we also began to suffer great loss. We lost our cars, our storage unit which housed the remainder of our personal belongings, and eventually, we were even evicted from our apartment. In all that transpired, my faith in who God was, was not shaken. God still proved Himself and was faithful in his promise to us; "I will take care of you." My family and I didn't see God's plan, but out of obedience to His commands, we were blessed to rise to a level of stability because we believed. The experience matured us in our faith.

146

Mature Faith Requires Mastering Trust

In Proverbs 3:5-6, we are told to "trust in the Lord with all your heart; and lean not unto your own understanding. In all your ways acknowledge Him, and He will direct your path." Trusting God would be easy if our minds did not present us with all of the alternatives to doing so. In order to master trusting God totally, we must be equipped with scripture and prepared to use it to combat doubt. Therefore, our response to a lack of faith is the repetition of and meditation on the Word of God. When Jesus was challenged by Satan after He had fasted in the wilderness (Matthew 4:1-11) His response to every attempt to derail His faith was the Word. It was the Word that halted Satan's assault. Likewise, Gideon needed a word or an assurance; he was desirous of a personal demonstration of the Word of which his ancestors spoke. Though receiving directions from God, Gideon then said to God, "Please don't be angry with me, but let me make one more request." We say, "God, can you just show me one more time?"

God's promises are not empty but full of life-giving grace and mercy. God fulfilling his promises also strengthens and grows our faith in Him to prove that His plan is trustworthy. Just as Isaiah 55:11 states. GOD's Word holds true, and we can be assured that what He says to us, He will do. Even when it looks so to our natural eyes, we can be sure that there is no failure in God. Everything He does is perfect, on purpose and with purpose.

We can all relate to Gideon; we have all been in Gideon's position at some point in our lives; we all have allowed fear to control or dictate our faith, we all have second-guessed whether to do the work God has ordained us to accomplish. This is simply an aspect of our humanity. God, however, calls us to live from a supernatural vantage point. Our faith must lead us. Lack of faith makes it difficult for us to see the plan God has for us. However, if we trust in God and demonstrate that by following His instructions, we will be able to accomplish the mission that is set before us.

Who Will You Be When Your Faith Grows Up?

Here is a profound question. Who will you be when your faith grows up? As believers, we must strive to walk in mature faith. What does it mean to be mature in our faith? It means that we have confidence that God will do exactly what He promised. Wavering and doubt are replaced with the bold confidence that accompanies the assurance that if God is for us, things will always materialize in our best interests and for His glory.

When our faith is matured, there is no need to ask God repeatedly for proof or numerous confirmations. His Word is confirmation enough, and it is the solid rock on which we build our hopes and settle our expectations. It is such confidence that empowers us to manifest destiny and reflect God's best through our lives. Gideon came to this place in much the same way we all do – trial and error. However, once he arrived, he was no longer confused about his purpose and destiny. His now matured faith fueled his prowess in battle and resolved that he was fighting for the right cause under the inspiration of the only true and living God. When we are mature in our faith, we too will simply trust and believe what God has spoken to us. Then we will carry out that which He has called or sent us to do. Mature faith is being assured of two things, one – He is and two - it is so.

Questions

1. Do you believe that every believer has a calling of God on their life? If so, what do you believe is your calling?

_____

_____

_____

_____

2. Do you believe that it is appropriate to fleece God? Why or why not?

_____

_____

_____

_____

3. Why is it that we sometimes need so much proof or evidence before we even consider doing what God asks of us?

_____

_____

_____

_____

4. What do you think it would take for you to trust and believe
    God at His Word?

    _____

    _____

    _____

5. Do you think that Gideon was looking for a way out of doing
    what God had called Him to do? Have you ever looked for a
    way out of what God was calling you to do?

    _____

    _____

    _____

    _____

6. What are some ways that you can develop your faith to a
    mature faith?

    _____

    _____

    _____

    _____

Chapter 9
Conceptualizing and Walking in Your Kingdom Identity
by Yasha Jones Becton

Prayer

Father, thank You that I AM fearfully and wonderfully made. Thank You for the plan that You had for my life before I was formed in my mother's womb. I submit to You. I submit to Your will for my life. Help me, Father, to walk in my true identity. Nothing more, but certainly nothing less.

In Jesus Name,
Amen

We conclude our discussion about your Kingdom identity with a look at how you can realistically and practically conceptualize and walk in your Kingdom identity. By conceptualize, we simply mean that you need to mentally grasp the big picture. If after reading this book, you remain confused about who you are or what your true identity is, then somehow this book would have missed the mark. This is why I believe God has given the release or the download of what is contained in this chapter.

Now, let's get to work. As you read this chapter, try not to think about anyone else. In other words, try not to disqualify yourself as you read the contents. In my time of prayer and meditation, the Holy Spirit revealed five key elements to conceptualizing your true identity. These areas include:

1) Your Jesus Calling
2) Your Grace Giftings
3) Your Kingdom Assignments
4) Your Defining Moments
5) Your Uniquely Divine Characteristics.

The Role of the Holy Spirit in Our Identity

In this chapter, we will examine these five key areas. Before we embark upon that journey, we need to explore the role of the Holy Spirit in our Kingdom identity. Apart from the Holy Spirit, we cannot fully walk in our Kingdom identity. Why? Because the Holy Spirit himself is the one who identifies who we are, the one who confirms who we are, and the one who teaches us how to operate in our true identity.

Remember that I shared there is no confusion in heaven about who you are. Your identity is settled in heaven and can only be disputed or dismissed in an earthly realm. In John 16:13 (KJV), the scripture states, "Howbeit when he, the Spirit of truth, is come, he will guide you into all truth: for he shall not speak of himself; but whatsoever he shall hear, that shall he speak: and he will shew you things to come". The Holy Spirit is privy to the heavenly conversations concerning you and only repeats to you what He hears. He can release to you the identity that God predestined for you to have. He hears, and He speaks.

To take this further, once He releases to you who you are, He is also able to teach you how to be that person. An experience so real and defining that the scripture states in I John 2:27 (NLT), "But you have received the Holy Spirit, and he lives within you, so you don't need anyone to teach you what is true. For the Spirit teaches you everything you need to know, and what he teaches is true-it is not a lie. So just as he has taught you, remain in fellowship with Christ". What an extremely powerful text! Once the Holy Spirit releases to you who you really are and the heavenly conversation that He hears about you, He can also serve as your teacher. His teaching skills are so profound that the scriptures state that you really don't need anyone else to teach you. This doesn't negate that fact that God has set up spiritual leaders that hold us accountable and are responsible for teaching and mentoring us. It also doesn't negate the fact that as the body of Christ, we are interdependent. What it is saying is that when it comes to your Kingdom identity, God does not shift the primary weight of this responsibility outside of the Trinity, and the Holy Spirit is the designated teacher. The Father declares who you are, the Son intercedes on your behalf, and the Holy Spirit teaches you how to be who God has called you to be.

When we understand this, we understand the anointing and what it means to be anointed. The anointing is simply the supernatural endowment of the Holy Spirit. The anointing of God on your life is Jesus-Centered, Others-Focused, and Eternally Significant. This leads me into our first discussion about "Your Jesus Calling."

What is "Your Jesus Calling"?

Isaiah 61:1-4

The Spirit of the Lord GOD is upon me; because the LORD hath anointed me to preach good tidings unto the meek; he hath sent me to bind up the brokenhearted, to proclaim liberty to the captives, and the opening of the prison to them that are bound; To proclaim the acceptable year of the LORD, and the day of vengeance of our God; to comfort all that mourn; To appoint unto them that mourn in Zion, to give unto them beauty for ashes, the oil of joy for mourning, the garment of praise for the spirit of heaviness; that they might be called trees of righteousness, the planting of the LORD, that he might be glorified.

Luke 4:18-20

The Spirit of the Lord is upon me, because he hath anointed me to preach the gospel to the poor; he hath sent me to heal the brokenhearted, to preach deliverance to the captives, and recovering of sight to the blind, to set at liberty them that are bruised, To preach the acceptable year of the Lord. And he closed the book, and he gave it again to the minister, and sat down. And the eyes of all them that were in the synagogue were fastened on him.

Here in these two scriptures, we have a very clear overview of what Jesus was called or anointed to do while He was on the Earth. It's so clear that it was referenced in both the Old Testament and the New Testament. Follow me. As believers of Christ, shouldn't our calling here on earth mirror or, at the very least, tap into the calling of Jesus. If so, it behooves us to understand His calling whereby which we can have assistance in identifying our own.

With that being said, there are three key essentials of Jesus' calling. It is important to bear in mind that they have eternal significance individually and collectively. This is important to understand because as earthly beings, we must prepare to wrap our minds around the things in the Kingdom of God that carry eternal significance.

3 Elements of Jesus Calling

1. **To Speak** – The first and, in some cases, the most obvious, Jesus was called to speak. Specifically, in the text referenced earlier, he was called to "preach good tidings unto the meek." He was also called to "proclaim the acceptable year of the Lord." As we talk about our Kingdom identity, some people have been uniquely gifted to speak. This can manifest in them serving as a preacher, teacher, writer, singer, and numerous other ways. The Holy

155

Spirit is not limited in how He can use our voices, the Word of God, the anointing of God, and the revelation of God to create and initiate eternal significance in the life of someone else.

2. **To Soothe** – Although it is not highlighted as much as some other areas, Jesus was also sent to soothe and bring comfort to the wounded. Although we celebrate those that are called to proclaim the Word of God, sometimes you need someone who is anointed to bring comfort. We see this in the description of Jesus' calling when it states that He was called to "bind up the brokenhearted" and "to appoint unto them that mourn in Zion, to give unto them beauty for ashes, the oil of joy for mourning...". Our Heavenly Father is ever-so-concerned about those that are hurting and in need of healing. Those anointed to demonstrate care and comfort are just as important as those who have been anointed to speak. In the scriptures, we find that He is described as "the Father of compassion and the God of all comfort, who comforts us in all our troubles so that we can comfort those in any trouble with the comfort we ourselves receive from God. For just as we share abundantly in the suffering of Christ, so also our comfort abounds through Christ." (2 Cor. 1:3-5 NIV). How we comfort and whether we comfort is a matter of eternal significance. Even if you are called and anointed to speak, understand that people are the only real emergency.

<u>One of the ways that God uses me when I'm ministering at the altar is simply by giving a hug</u>. I only offer a hug when I prompted by the Holy Spirit, but when I do the Holy Spirit comforts the person I'm holding. Some people don't need another message. They don't really want to hear what you have to say. Think about it, when you are in excruciating pain, do you want to hold a conversation with anyone. I certainly don't. Sometimes people are before us and around us, but their hearts are completely broken. They need to experience the Love of the Father.

3. **To Set Free** – Then there are those in the Body of Christ who are anointed to liberate others. Part of Jesus' assignment was to "proclaim liberty to the captives and the opening of the prisons to those that are bound." The anointing of God comes to set us free from the weight of guilt or the weight of sin. It comes to set us free from the traditions of men. It comes to set us free from the dysfunction and bondage of our past. The scripture proclaims that where the Spirit of the Lord is there is liberty. There is freedom.

As you read this, there are some of you who may be gifted in all three areas, and then there are some of you who can clearly see yourself in one particular area. The key here is to understand that part of your identity should include what I've termed "Your Jesus Calling." And you should be able to clearly articulate what the anointing of God looks like on you. When you are able to do so, it doesn't mean that you lack humility, instead, it means that you have gained clarity. Just as we explored in the faith chapter, who will you be when your faith grows up. We also seek to understand who are you when the anointing of God hits your life. This is a significant part of your Kingdom identity.

What is Your Grace Giftings?

Ephesians 4:1-16 *King James Version (KJV)*
I therefore, the prisoner of the Lord, beseech you that ye walk worthy of the vocation wherewith ye are called, With all lowliness and meekness, with longsuffering, forbearing one another in love; Endeavouring to keep the unity of the Spirit in the bond of peace. There is one body, and one Spirit, even as ye are called in one hope of your calling; One Lord, one faith, one baptism,
One God and Father of all, who is above all, and through all, and in you all. But unto every one of us is given grace according to the measure of the gift of Christ. Wherefore he saith, When he ascended up on high, he led captivity captive, and gave gifts unto men. (Now that he ascended, what is it but that he also descended first into the lower parts of the Earth? He that descended is the same also that ascended up far above all heavens, that he might fill all things.)
And he gave some, apostles; and some, prophets; and some, evangelists; and some, pastors and teachers; For the perfecting of the saints, for the work of the ministry, for the edifying of the body of Christ: Till we all come in the unity of the faith, and of the knowledge of the Son of God, unto a perfect man, unto the measure of the stature of the fulness of Christ: That we henceforth be no more children, tossed to and fro, and carried about with every wind of doctrine, by the sleight of men, and cunning craftiness, whereby they lie in wait to deceive; But speaking the truth in love, may grow up into him in all things, which is the head, even Christ: From whom the whole body fitly joined together and compacted by that which every joint supplieth, according to the

effectual working in the measure of every part, maketh increase of the body unto the edifying of itself in love.

Romans 12:3-9

For I say, through the grace given unto me, to every man that is among you, not to think of himself more highly than he ought to think; but to think soberly, according as God hath dealt to every man the measure of faith. For as we have many members in one body, and all members have not the same office: So we, being many, are one body in Christ, and every one members one of another. Having then gifts differing according to the grace that is given to us, whether prophecy, let us prophesy according to the proportion of faith; Or ministry, let us wait on our ministering: or he that teacheth, on teaching; Or he that exhorteth, on exhortation: he that giveth, let him do it with simplicity; he that ruleth, with diligence; he that sheweth mercy, with cheerfulness. Let love be without dissimulation. Abhor that which is evil; cleave to that which is good.

To further understand our Kingdom identity, we must understand that there are certain gifts that we are graced to do in the Kingdom. Ephesians 4 and Romans 12 are good places to start the process of prayerfully seeking God about what you have been both gifted and graced to do in the Kingdom of God.

I like that in each of the scriptural texts, grace is a centerpiece. Except for the grace or the unmerited favor of God, we could not even have the discussion related to a Kingdom Identity. I like when Paul says in I Corinthians 15:10, "But by the grace of God I am what I am, and his grace which was bestowed upon me was not in vain: but I labored more abundantly than they all: yet not I, but the grace of God which was with me." As you begin to pull this picture together of who you are in the Kingdom of God, remember it's only by the grace of God. None of us is any better than any one of us, and all of us need His grace.

This reality is designed to keep us in a humble posture before the Father. It's okay to recognize that you have been gifted to serve in a particular area or do a particular thing, but it's equally important that you recognize you had nothing to do with the fact that you were gifted with certain gifts. Again, we can call on the Apostle Paul to bring clarity, I Corinthians 4:7 states, "For who maketh thee to differ from another? And what hast thou that thou didst not receive? Now if thou didst receive it, why dost thou glory, as if thou hast not received it?" In other words, who has given you your unique Kingdom Identity? God, of course. You had absolutely nothing to do it. Since you had nothing to do it, do not get the big head or behave in a way that gives you a distinction or clout above the next person. There is no need for you or me to glory in it or walk according to the pride of our flesh.

I love how the scriptures state in Luke 4:20 how Jesus read the scripture and then handed the Word back to the minister and sat down. It is basically like they looked at him like he was crazy. Listen, when your identity is smothered in clarity and settled in heaven, the dispute may be around you, but it is certainly not in you. You can offer clarity to those that will accept it and then take a seat. Again, we are not here to prove anything other than what is that good, acceptable, and perfect will of God.

Providing Further Definition to Your Kingdom Identity

There are three additional areas that have some degree of influence as we talk about our Kingdom Identity. These areas are Your Kingdom Assignments, Your Defining Moments, and Your UDCs (I'll explain in a few). So much goes into who you are in the Kingdom of God.

When we speak of Your Kingdom Assignments, we are talking specifically about what God has assigned to your hands to do. We see in the Old Testament various assignments explained with tremendous detail. When you think about Noah and the Ark or even Solomon as it relates to the Temple, thorough instructions were provided. We can also move forward to the New Testament and attest to the fact that God was still not short on providing instructions or issuing assignments. We can see this clearly with the 12 disciples and the Apostle Paul, along with many others.

The fact of the matter is, you have Kingdom Assignments as well. My Kingdom Assignments include serving as a wife, a mother, and a writer, to name a few. I purposely included my role as a wife and a mother, because often we don't see these roles and responsibilities as "spiritual" or "Kingdom" related. Trust me, they are. I remember when I first became a parent, the Holy Spirit asked me one simple question: "Can I trust you with a soul?" I almost fainted in the Wal-Mart parking lot because I understood both the weight and the ramifications of the question. After gathering myself and my thoughts, I simply replied, "Lord, thou knowest." At the moment, I did not want to be presumptuous in my answer. As you conceptualize your Kingdom Identity, think about what God has assigned to your hands. Also, think about who God has assigned to your hands.

In addition to your Kingdom Assignments, there will be Defining Moments. Moments that occur in your life that begin to shape or further identify who you are. As believers, we are challenged not to allow anything to negatively affect us to the degree that it distorts or causes us to abandon who God created us to be. However, there are certain times and instances in life when what we go through and what we walk through define us. They become the lessons learned that we take with us throughout our lifetime.

Lastly, there are UDCs or Uniquely Divine Characteristics, the fingerprint of God on your life that makes you uniquely you. There is no one like you in the whole Earth. Think about that.

Walking in Your God-sized identity

Guess what? It's time for you to put what you've learned into practice. It's time for you to be the person that God has created you to be. The Body of Christ needs you. The world needs you.

CULMINATING ASSIGNMENT

DIRECTIONS: In lieu of questions, we would like for you to create a statement about your God-sized identity. As you reflect on what is outlined in this chapter and the book overall, fill in the blanks below and begin the process of clearly articulating your God-sized identity. I'm sharing GSIPS (God-sized identity Personal Statement) with you as an example.

(To be Completed)
Creating My "God-Sized" Identity

My name is _____. I am 100% wholeheartedly committed to walking in my "God-Sized" identity. My Jesus Calling is _____ _____. My

Jesus Calling is most evident when I _____.

My graced gifts include the gifts of _____.

My Kingdom Assignment is to _____.

I recognize that I am fearfully and wonderfully made. I am unique in terms of_____

I am uniquely gifted to

_____.

One defining moment in my life was when _____.

This   defining   moment   taught   me   how   to _____. Now, at the age of _____, my goal is to redeem the time and maximize my potential by walking in my God-sized identity. I offer no apologies to anyone for walking in my God-sized identity. Even if my God-sized identity makes others uncomfortable. I will encourage them to pursue their God-sized identity. I will secure mentors that see me as God sees me and are willing to help me remain committed to this journey. I will not judge myself prematurely, nor allow others to do so. I will not compare myself to others, nor allow others to do so. I will hold myself to the standard of my God-sized identity. Thank you, Father, for creating me and allowing me to be an example of you in the Earth. Because of you, I have been Properly Id'd.

SAMPLE

Creating My "God-Sized" Identity

My name is Yasha Jones Becton. I am 100% wholeheartedly committed to walking in my "God-Sized" identity. My Jesus Calling is threefold – it is to speak, to soothe, and to set free. My Jesus Calling is most evident when I minister the Word of God or minister a word of encouragement or healing to someone in need. My graced gifts include the gifts of teaching, administration, prophecy, and exhortation. My Kingdom Assignment is to walk as a mouthpiece and Prophet of God, specifically as a prophetic scribe and prophetic intercessor.

I recognize that I am fearfully and wonderfully made. I am unique in terms of my perspective, my introverted personality, my professional and educational background, and my insatiable love for people (especially children). I am uniquely gifted to generate generations. Generate means to cause to arise or come about.

One defining moment in my life was when my brother passed away unexpectedly at the age of 50. This defining moment taught me how to trust God in all things.

Now, at the age of 48, my goal is to redeem the time and maximize my potential by walking in my God-sized identity. I offer no apologies, to anyone for walking in my true identity. Even if my

God-sized identity makes others feel uncomfortable. I will encourage them to pursue their God-sized identity.

I will secure mentors that see me as God sees me and are willing to help me remain committed to this journey. I will not judge myself prematurely nor allow others to do so. I will not compare myself to others nor allow others to do so. I will hold myself to the standard of my God-sized identity. Thank you, Father, for creating me and allowing me to be an example of you in the Earth. Because of you, I have been Properly Id'd.

About the Authors

Kristen Baker

Kristen D. Baker is an influential millennial leader. She is a minister of the gospel whether through the preached word, music, conferences, concerts, or books. Kristen is also an entrepreneur and a South Carolina realtor. Kristen's motto is to blaze trails and build bridges. She is committed to heralding the fact that God speaks and that our lives are exponentially better as a result of following His voice.

Gary Becton

Apostle Gary Becton is a native of Durham, North Carolina and the son of the late Percy and the Reverend Johnnie Mae Becton. After serving in the United States Marine Corp., Apostle Becton attended Coastal Carolina Community College and North Carolina State University. Apostle Gary was officially ordained and licensed to the office of Prophet, by Apostle Willie S. Darden at The Word of God Deliverance Evangelist Church, in Enfield NC, in 2009. In 2010, God gave him the mandate to begin God's End Time Warriors Apostolic Ministries. It was at this time that Apostle Becton accepted the call and the mandate to teach fivefold ministry leaders and other mature believers how to adequately prepare for the end times. In 2013, Apostle Becton answered the call to the Apostleship. Currently, Apostle Becton serves as the CEO of God's End Time Warriors Apostolic and Prophetic Ministries and the Overseer of Revealing Word Ministries. Apostle Gary Becton is married to Dr. Yasha Jones Becton of Columbia, South Carolina. Together, they are delighted to have three sons, one daughter, and one granddaughter. To contact Apostle Becton, please email him at getwministry@gmail.com.

GOD'S END TIME WARRIORS

Apostolic *Ministry*

School of the Prophets

Ushering in the Glory Prophetic Conference

Dr. Yasha Becton
Vice President

Apostle Gary Becton
Founder & President

Spiritual Seminars & Workshops

Spiritual Counseling for Fivefold Ministry Gifts

GOD'S END TIME WARRIORS

APOSTOLIC MINISTRY

Preaching the Kingdom
Reaching the World
Matthew 24:13-14

Yasha Jones Becton

 **Yasha Jones Becton** is the founder and Co-Pastor of Revealing Word Ministries of Columbia, SC where she serves alongside her husband Apostle Gary Becton. Revealing Word Ministries is a ministry uniquely designed to help believers and unbelievers understand and respond to the glorious gospel of Jesus Christ. Initially licensed as an Evangelist in 2001 by the Church of God in Christ, Dr. Becton accepted the call of God and the responsibility to preach and teach the Word of God to a myriad of audiences. Educationally, she matriculated through Richland District One schools. She holds a Doctor of Education degree in Curriculum and Instruction from the University of South Carolina and Master of Education degrees from Columbia College and the University of South Carolina. Currently, she serves as a Clinical Assistant Professor with her alma mater, USC. She also serves as the founder and CEO of Wysdom Central Publications, LLC. A Christian publishing company focused on igniting a flame for God's Word and God's Wisdom. Dr. Becton is the daughter of Mr. Harvey Jones and Ms. Patricia Sullivan. Together, Dr. Becton and Apostle Gary Becton have a daughter by the name of Angel, three adult sons, and one granddaughter.

Ebony Green

Ebony Green is the founder and CEO of Business and Books, LLC and a proud South Carolina native. Business and Books, LLC has helped numerous *Christian* schools, authors, ministries and entrepreneurs (S.A.M.E.) market and brand God's way through the company's course, Market **ME** *–God* ™. Business and Books, LLC also promotes unity in the Body of Christ and the marketplace with their app, The **KING**dom Directory (available on Google Play store).

Ebony has pegged herself as "God's Businesswoman™." Similar to the company's motto, she is all *about the Father's business*. Her education includes an undergraduate degree in English-Literature. A Master of Education Degree in Early Childhood and Childhood Education, and a Juris Doctor degree. In 2019, the U.S. Commission on Civil Rights appointed her to a four-year term for the S.C. Advisory Committee Board. She is also one of *The 2019 Whole Truth Magazine's* 40 under 40.

In addition to business, Ebony is also a licensed minister and has been affirmed to the office of the Prophet. Her personal ministry is "Hands and Feet Ministries ~ Breaking the Walls of Tradition." She is also the founder of The Make Things Move Campaign, a prayer line for Christ believing women. Within her local church, she serves as the Young Adult Chair and on the prayer team for Victorious Believers Ministries C.O.G.I.C. For booking, please email booking@businessbooksllc.com.

God's Businesswoman™

EBONY GREEN

KINGdom Directory App

NOW AVAILABLE

| VISION PLANNING | CLERGY | BUSINESS CONSULTING | APPAREL |

IDENTITY CRISIS SERIES

Contact

9005 Two Notch Road Columbia, SC 29223
*By Appt Only/Travel Locally & Abroad
(803)250-5374
booking@businessbooksllc.com
www.businessandbooksllc.com

f **⊙** Godsbusinesswoman

BOOKS AVAILABLE VIA SITE

Kylie McBride

Kylie McBride presents an experienced, empathetic, and relevant voice in relationship to pertinent matters of the heart. Having lived through and prospered in spite of the tremendous pain of sexual abuse, Kylie offers a firsthand perspective on rebuilding, recovering and reaching one's highest potential.

Kylie's first book, *Leaving My Brother's House*, chronicles her ongoing transformational journey as she confronts the trauma of childhood sexual abuse. Her transparency is intended to break the cycle of secrecy that prevents healing and justice.

Kylie holds a Bachelor of Arts in English from Coker College, a Master's in Pastoral Counseling and a Master of Divinity from Liberty University. She also holds a Graduate Certificate in Marriage and Family Therapy from Capella University.

She serves as the Senior Pastor of **An Invitation to Prayer Outreach Ministries** in Columbia, South Carolina, which she founded in 2014. She is the proud mother of one daughter, Bethany.

Shawn Moreland

Prophetess Shawn Moreland is a woman of God who first and foremost, loves and honors God. Prophetess Moreland is also a native of Trenton, New Jersey. She is the loving daughter of the late John Alford and Sheila Moreland. Uniquely gifted to serve women, children, families and senior citizens, professionally she serves as a counselor, life skills specialist and family care specialist. Prophetess Shawn positions herself as a servant of God with a sincere heart and love for people. She is the founder of "Matters of the Heart" ministries which is an outreach ministry designed to meet the needs of teens and young adults. Ministering to youth in crisis, recovering mothers and families, as well as youth in foster care are especially near and dear to her heart. Within her local church Prophetess Moreland serves as the leader of the South Carolina Chapter of the King's Daughters Ministry. Prophetess Shawn loves God and she also loves being a mother to her two young adult children: Brittany and Jovan. Next to God, family and helping others means everything. Her daily prayer is to make a difference in the lives of others one day at a time in order that God may be glorified.

Dr. Gert Thompson

Dr. Gert Thompson serves as the Senior Pastor of Life Changing Ministries of Irmo, SC. Dr. Thompson has served this ministry for over forty years in music, teaching, counseling as well as pastoring for eighteen years. As a prolific minister of the gospel and ordained Prophet of God, she serves the body of Christ through teaching, equipping and evangelizing. Dr. Thompson has given countless hours to many community endeavors. These endeavors include establishing an offsite Bible Study at a local homeless shelter, facilitating workshops for neighboring churches, and serving as a conference speaker.

Educationally: Dr. Thompson earned her Associate Degree in Fashion Design and her Bachelor's Degree in Biblical Studies. Dr. Thompson also received a Master's of Pastoral Ministry, a Master's of Divinity and a Doctorate of Ministry. She is affiliated with the Columbia Pentecostal Fellowship and a Community Advocate for Palmetto Richland Parkridge Hospital.

Dr. Gert Thompson is the widowed, mother of one son and four beautiful granddaughters. She has passionately coined the phrase, "If I am not willing to do God's will, then I don't need to be alive." To contact Pastor Thompson, please email her at trudence@bellsouth.net.

Made in the USA
Middletown, DE
11 January 2026

26762058R10106